1st LOAD OF LOGS LEAVING
THE SNOW PEAK CAMP FOR
THE POND   July 1939

MAKING THE MOST OF THE BEST

Making the Most of the Best

Willamette Industries' Seventy-Five Years

by

Catherine A. Baldwin

Published By
Willamette Industries, Inc.
Portland, Oregon

Publisher:
Willamette Industries, Inc.
3800 First Interstate Tower
Portland, Oregon 97201

Library of Congress catalog number 82-70740
Printed in the United States of America

Table of Contents

Willamette Industries, Inc. is a 14-year-old entity, but its heritage dates back to 1906 when its parent company, Willamette Valley Lumber Co., was formed.

This is a book about a pioneer venture, started as a railroading and farm land development concern, that evolved first into lumbering; then into the production of plywood, pulp and paper, particleboard, corrugated containers, paper bags, folding cartons and business forms. The single uniform thread in its development has been the forest and the renewable fiber it provides.

As chronicled in this book, many critical periods and many fortunate events meshed for this independent company to survive 75 years and become a respected, publicly-owned, fully-integrated forest products company with 60 manufacturing facilities in 14 states.

The foresight, tenacity, risk-taking and imagination of company leaders, along with the skills and loyalties of thousands of employees, advisors and supporters, have made the company a success.

It is impossible to name everyone who made a significant contribution to the company's development and for those omitted, the record of Willamette is just as much a tribute to your efforts as to those identified.

Records were somewhat thin on various eras and undoubtedly there are some errors and omissions. On balance, the book is a reasonably accurate history of a great company.

Gene D. Knudson

September 15, 1981

Acknowledgements

In 1975 Willamette's management embarked upon a project that would culminate in the printing of a corporate history on the company's 75th anniversary. Dave James, a highly respected writer and a recent retiree of Simpson, was hired to interview company employees and retirees and compile oral histories. His completed project was turned over to the Oregon Historical Society. Charles Digregorio of the Society did a second round of oral histories, then cataloged the historical documents available in company archives.

Late in 1978 the company began the search for an author. After several false starts, it was determined the book should be done internally and Cathy Baldwin, the company's corporate communications manager, was chosen to write the history.

There was very little information in the company's archives about the Willamette Valley Lumber Co. from 1901 to 1945 (when Van Reidy joined the company as secretary to Bill Swindells and began to keep scrap books). The oral histories compiled by James and the Historical Society were supplemented by copious news articles from the *Polk County Itemizer,* the *Polk County Observer* and *The Timberman.* Doreen Portal, head reference librarian for the Western Oregon State College in Monmouth, was of tremendous help to the author in the research stage.

From there, Aaron Mercer, Glenn Stevens and Harry Davis took over, advising the author on the early days of logging and railroading. Maurie Clark, Ed Cutler, Ted Huntley and the Swindells family were primary references for early-day sawmilling chapters. Neil Duffie, Dick Keller and Bill Knodell were the guides through the Paper Group formation; Sam Wheeler, through the Building Materials Group development in the South.

Ann Hertzberg and Cheryl DeHart typed many of the drafts, assisted by Rhonda Simmons, Judy Timm, Charlene Leep and Peggy Hansen. They not only did the typing, they reminded the author that not all readers know the definition of "choker setter" or "flexo".

Dan Kieft, Elmo Richardson and Robert S. Miller helped with the over-all review of the book.

Ted Huntley, Aaron Mercer and Rex Pemberton performed an immeasurable service to the company by identifying and cataloging photos.

The company also owes Bill Paxson a debt of gratitude for keeping the company's few historical files and photographs under lock and key and for developing a rough dateline of the company's significant events.

C.A.B.

CHAPTER 1

The Salem, Falls City and Western Railway Company

Willamette Industries, Inc. celebrated its seventy-fifth anniversary in 1980. During that year, Willamette employed 8,500 men and women in fourteen states, making lumber, plywood, veneer, particleboard, pulp, paper, corrugated containers, bags, business forms and folding cartons; a successful corporation by any man's standard.

Time and fate have a way of toying with the goals of corporations. Opportunities and risks taken lead to a labyrinth of new choices. Goals reached often differ dramatically from the course set. Such was the case with Willamette. In 1901 when Louis Gerlinger, Sr. began to buy timberland in Polk County, Oregon, he wanted to construct a cargo and passenger railway and to sell cut-over lands to homesteaders. His goals were simple and realistic for the era. The end result of his endeavors, Willamette Industries, Inc., was far beyond his dreams.

II

Louis Gerlinger, Sr. became involved in the railroad business comparatively late in life. He was born in Alsace-Lorraine (a region between France and Germany) in 1853. At the age of 17, he came to the United States, settling in Chicago. He married, fathered three sons and a daughter and built a prosperous store and saloon fixture business.

At 41, Gerlinger left his comfortable, successful Chicago enterprise to move his family West. He settled in the Portland, Oregon area and in 1896 organized and built the Portland, Vancouver and Yakima Railroad on behalf of the Harrimans.

In the fall of 1901 Gerlinger purchased 7,000 acres of timberland in Polk County, Oregon for a railroad. Just west of Dallas (the county seat of Polk County, located 63 miles south of Portland) in the Coast Range Mountains, grew hundreds of square miles of Douglas fir and other commercial timber species, untouched by the iron horse and the cross-cut saw.

He incorporated the Salem, Falls City and Western Railway Company late in October of 1901 and announced plans to build a railroad from the Willamette River at Salem to the mouth of the Siletz River on the Oregon Coast, a distance of 65 miles.

Within a week of the incorporation, the Salem and Pacific Coast Railway Company presented another proposal to the Dallas Board of Trade for a railway from the valley into the timber. The new company said they would build their railroad through Dallas if the townsfolk pledged a $10,000 bonus to be claimed upon completion of the railroad from the north-south Southern Pacific line east of Dallas to Falls City, some 9 miles west.

Knowing that development of those timberlands was key to the town's future, the Board of Trade agreed to raise $10,000 by subscription from residents of Dallas, to be paid to any company that completed the railroad within one year.

The Salem, Falls City and Western appeared to be the most serious contender. But things on both sides went far from smoothly. By April of 1902 the citizens of Dallas had raised only $5,000, their enthusiasm for the subscription program dampened by the fact that they could see no progress on the railroad. Hampered by delays in obtaining equipment, the Company had postponed construction.

The contract was renegotiated between Dallas and the Salem, Falls City and Western, with Dallas to furnish only a $5,000 bonus plus terminal grounds for the railway and four miles of right-of-way. The new bargain was sealed and a carload of plows, scrapers and other grading implements soon arrived.

Work began in earnest in September 1902. The Company was required to complete the railroad before June 6, 1903 to claim the bonus, necessitating working through Oregon's rainy season. One hundred men and fifty teams labored that fall and winter in a race against time and weather.

Steel rails were imported from Belgium because of a one-year backlog in orders for American steel. About 900 tons of rail were brought from Europe, at a hefty import duty, to complete the railway on time.

On May 29, just eight days before the required completion date, the first train ran from Dallas to Falls City.

At the end of June, passenger trains began regularly scheduled trips to and from Dallas and Falls City each day; the nine-mile, forty-minute, one-way trip costing 35 cents.

Gerlinger's two sons, George and Louis, Jr., managed the railway.

III

But the system was far from complete. Crews began a logging railroad from Falls City into the Coast Range timber in December 1904. Demand for lumber was tremendous, and the tracks between Falls City and Dallas were the busiest of any Oregon railroad.

Four miles of rails were punched into the timber. J.C. Hayter, a local editor and publisher, described the railway's path:

> . . . the road plunges into the rock-walled canyon of the Luckiamute River and follows the meanderings of that beautiful stream for a distance of two miles. The scenery is rugged and wild beyond description, the river flowing swiftly between the banks densely covered with timber and the mountains rising to dizzy heights on either side.

The road's end was a brand-new logging town—Black Rock.

IV

Louis Gerlinger, Sr. became a walking Chamber of Commerce for Polk County and soon began attracting investors. In 1904 he induced two groups of capitalists to build an oak sawmill and a handle factory on the Dallas terminal grounds.

A year later, George Gerlinger announced plans for a "first class mill" west of Falls City. The Falls City Lumber Co., with a 60,000 board foot per day capacity, began operating in July 1905.

Just a few months later, George Cone, another investor recruited by Gerlinger, began construction of a second sawmill on the terminal grounds in Dallas.

In 1906 the Salem, Falls City and Western published a prospectus indicating its net annual earnings to be $19,500 for freight, passenger and mail service. Further, it spoke of opportunities in the area tapped by the railway:

> Immediately west of Falls City, and adjacent to the line of Railway as now located, there are five townships of the finest standing

timber in the Pacific Northwest. This is composed largely of Yellow Fir, Larch, Cedar and Hemlock, the trees usually ranging from two to seven feet in diameter, and from 150 to 250 feet in height—7,000,000 feet of marketable timber to the quarter section is a very fair average. It is estimated that there is in this body of timber not less than Four and One-half Billion (4,500,000,000) feet, board measure, all of which is accessible to the Railway by extending the main line and the building of short spur lines. Most of this land is elegant stock raising and farm land after the timber has been cut off.

V

By 1907 the railroad was thirteen miles long. It ran three geared and two rod locomotives and sixty cars, and was said to have more cars per mile of roadbed than any other Oregon railway. Dallas citizens were satisfied with the length of the railroad. They wanted nothing to do with an extension of the track east to Salem. They declared they were interested in "roads leading into Dallas, not out of it".

But the line was extended from Dallas to West Salem on the west bank of the Willamette River in 1908. Passengers and freight were ferried across the river to Salem by boat. Logs were dumped in the Willamette River to be floated to sawmills and paper mills down stream. However, the transfer of passengers and cargo during the rainy season became pretty exciting at times, so the Salem, Falls City and Western made application with the State to build a bridge across the Willamette River into Salem.

In August 1912 just after materials arrived and a contractor was hired to begin work on the bridge, the passenger portion of the railway—the 27 miles between Black Rock and West Salem—was sold to the Southern Pacific Railroad. The Gerlinger interests retained the logging railroad above Black Rock.

By the time of the sale, both Louis, Sr. and Louis, Jr. had moved on to other enterprises. The sale of the railroad left George to concentrate on the sawmilling, logging and timber interests of the family.

An advertisement for the Salem, Falls City and Western Railway that appeared in the Columbia River and
Oregon Timberman, *circa 1905*.

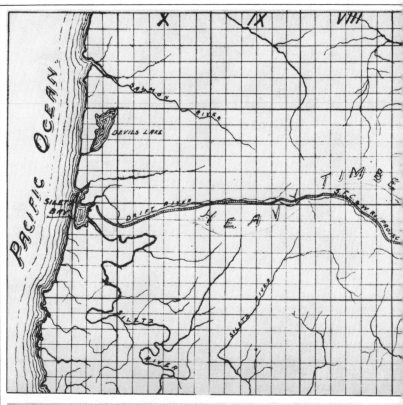

The proposed route of the Salem, Falls City and West-
ern Railway from a January 1, 1906 prospectus.

The Salem, Falls City and Western's Falls City terminals circa 1905. The terminals consisted of five acres, a depot, turntable and side tracks. Photo source: Cal Barnhart.

CHAPTER 2

The Development of the Willamette Valley Lumber Co.

George T. Gerlinger moved west with his father in 1896 at 20 years of age. While Louis, Sr.'s interests were in railroading, George's interests were in logging and sawmilling. George's first Western venture was a small logging operation near Yacolt, Washington, some 35 miles north of Portland. He was said to have introduced the first steam donkey engine to the area (a donkey engine was used to drag logs to an area where they could be loaded onto a railcar).

In 1902 one of the worst fires in the Pacific Northwest, the 238,920 acre Yacolt fire, burned out George's logging operation. He took a vacation in Europe, then returned to Oregon and bought an interest in the Deep Creek Lumber Co. in Clackamas County, just south of Portland.

By that time Louis, Sr. had built the first leg of his Salem, Falls City and Western Railway, and George took an increasing interest in the timberlands to be tapped by that railroad in the Coast Range. Soon he divested his interest in Deep Creek, and in 1905 he and several other investors built the Falls City Lumber Co., just west of Falls City, to process Coast Range logs. George Gerlinger managed the mill.

II

In 1905 Louis, Sr. encouraged George Cone to build the Cone Lumber Co. on the terminal grounds of the Salem, Falls City and Western in Dallas. Just two months after the mill sawed its first logs, in March 1906, the Gerlingers, H.L. Pittock and F.W. Leadbetter (two prominent West Coast lumbermen) purchased Cone Lumber. They bought the mill, 1,200 acres of timberland, three donkey engines and miscellaneous logging equipment for $50,000. The Cone mill, plus the Salem, Falls City and Western Railway and the Gerlingers' timberlands became the Willamette Valley Lumber Co. Louis Gerlinger, Sr. was president of the new company; H.L. Pittock, vice president; George T. Gerlinger, secretary / manager;

F.W. Leadbetter, treasurer; and George Cone, director and mill superintendent.

During its first year of operation, Willamette Valley Lumber Co. (WVLCo.) employed 40 men producing 60,000 board feet on a 10-hour shift.

Various projects increased the size and efficiency of the mill and by 1910 it was cutting 100,000 board feet on a 10-hour shift. That year, sales of lumber, slabwood, lath, shingles and moldings totaled $257,813.51. The mill made an average profit of $3.30 per thousand board feet of lumber produced.

One of the local papers, *The Polk County Observer,* nicknamed the mill "Old Reliable" because it ran regardless of economic conditions, unusual in the lumber industry of the era.

III

George Gerlinger married Irene Hazard and the couple had three daughters. He became active in community affairs in Dallas and was deeply involved in industry trade associations. His railroad background made him a key committee member on many lumbermen's association rail rate committees. He lobbied the State Legislature for the formation of the Oregon State Board of Forestry and for improvements in logging safety requirements. In 1913 Governor Oswald West appointed him as the State's representative to the nation's Fifth Conservation Congress. He served for years as an officer of the Willamette Valley Lumbermen's Association (a local sawmill-owners trade association).

George Gerlinger's growing prominence in industry affairs put him in the middle of one of the most bizarre chapters of labor and lumber history.

When World War I broke out in Europe, lumber was needed desperately for airplanes and ocean-going vessels. When the United States entered the war in 1917, the Pacific Northwest cranked up its sawmills to a fever pitch, with a full 70% of production going directly to the war effort.

The military draft took a bite out of the labor force, making it difficult to find mill and woods workers. As a result, the work force consisted mainly of foreigners and men over forty-five. It was a perfect set-up for the entrance of a union called the Industrial Workers of the World (IWW).

The IWW (called the "Wobblies" by some and the "I Won't Works" by others) was organized just after the turn of the century and took a foothold in the Pacific Northwest. IWW members wanted better working conditions and an eight hour day and were ready to use violence to get "money-hungry" employers to listen.

Its members would crop up in communities, commit acts of sabotage and violence, then leave. (They never left voluntarily. If they were lucky, the local sheriff ushered them out of town. If they were unlucky, they might be tarred and feathered and run out of town on a rail or even lynched.) Mills were sabotaged. Workers who would not join the IWW were threatened or beaten.

As the available workforce grew smaller, the IWW grew stronger.

The summer of 1917 was a dry one and the IWW made the most of it. Mill owners fighting fires, they reasoned, could not be producing lumber. With military orders for lumber piling up, owners might be willing to cooperate with the IWW for "fire protection".

Early in August a fire definitely linked to sabotage broke out in northwest Oregon. In mid-August the residents of Black Rock, just above Falls City, noticed wisps of smoke coming from WVLCo. timberlands.

Logging employees rushed to the scene and found a fire burning one of the Company's railroad trestles. The flames had just been extinguished when firefighters noticed smoke some distance away. A second fire was discovered burning near one of the Company's donkey engines. It would have been logical to conclude that the logging operation started the fire. However, the donkey engine had not been used for some time.

While sabotage could not be proven beyond a shadow of a doubt, it nonetheless appeared a strong possibility the fire was a result of IWW efforts.

The fire spread quickly. Families in the Company's logging camp, Balderee Camp, were rushed to Black Rock on flat cars with the few possessions they could gather before fire consumed the camp. The fire came so close to the retreating families they had to shield their faces from the intense heat. For a while it looked as though neighboring logging camps and even the town of Black Rock might fall victim to the fast-spreading flames.

All of the Company's loggers, loggers of neighboring companies and 30 mill men worked day and night to control the fire. The Balderee Camp, several donkey engines, railroad equipment and several railroad trestles were consumed by fire within two days. Total estimate of equipment loss alone was over $200,000.

The flames were contained after a few days. But in less than a week, fire broke out again and veered toward Dallas' water supply intake. Dallas' Mayor C.B. Stone led a brigade of businessmen to the woods in an onslaught against the flames. The town of Dallas was virtually deserted and logging and sawmilling in surrounding Polk County ground to a halt.

Oregon's Governor Withycombe announced he would send special detectives to the woods in search of arsonists. He also asked the military to send troops to patrol Oregon's forests to stop incendiary fires.

Finally the Oregon rains licked the arson problem. But it was obvious that something had to be done on the labor front to prevent a repetition of the 1917 fire season.

The Balderee Camp fire was not the only suspicious blaze on WVLCo. lands. Management was certain there had been repeated attempts to sabotage both the mill and the woods by fire.

Interruptions like these were contributing to delays in production of supplies for the nation's war effort, so Colonel Brice P. Disque, commander of the Spruce Division of the U.S. Signal Corps, moved to the Northwest to straighten things out. The Spruce Division had been organized by the military to provide manpower to log spruce, a critical component of aircraft.

Disque formed the Loyal Legion of Loggers and Lumbermen, a government-controlled union. It enrolled both employers and employees who jointly made decisions about labor questions on a 50-50 basis with Disque as arbitrator in case of dispute.

The Loyal Legion was a military-style organization with local chapters and a central committee of eight key employers and eight workers representing all areas of the Northwest. Throughout the Great War, George Gerlinger was one of the eight employer-advisors on Disque's central committee and chairman of the Loyal Legion's district committee. All WVLCo. employees were actively involved in Loyal Legion programs.

In retrospect, Disque's influence and accomplishments were formidable. He cajoled crusty employers who had fought the eight hour day for years into accepting it immediately. He required reasonable living conditions in logging camps and instituted a universal pay scale for work classifications to prevent loggers and mill workers from switching employers for better pay and conditions (and thus losing a day or more of production). "A day's lay-off is two days' work for the Kaiser" was one of his slogans.

Doing a good job became a patriotic duty. Many mills and camps had "closed shop" and refusal to join the Loyal Legion was a symbol of disloyalty and cause for immediate dismissal. Disque literally had men looking for saboteurs behind every tree.

Within one year the Loyal Legion had 100,000 members wearing its red, white and blue membership pins. Fires and other acts of sabotage stopped as the group routed out IWW sympathizers.

When World War I ended, this amazing chapter of lumbering labor history came to a close. But Gerlinger and the other central committee members convinced the industry to maintain the Loyal Legion as a peace-time labor union to insure strides made in labor relations were not lost.

The Willamette Valley Lumber Co. sawmill circa 1906.

The Willamette Valley Lumber Co. sawmill circa 1912.

The Willamette Valley Lumber Co. sawmill circa 1912.

PORTLAND, OREGON,

March 3rd, 1906

Mr L. Gerlinger
Portland Or

Dear Sir

We propose to sell you for your
corporation our mill property, timber lands with
timber, camps, logging engines & tools as follows

	$12000.00
Talbot tract 800 acres	2400.00
Ellis " 240 "	1000.00
Hinshaw " 80 "	1300.00
Van Orsdel " 80 "	
1 Willamette Iron Works 10 X 13 Donkey) including wire Ropes	
1 " " 8½ X 10 ")	10000.00
1 " " 5 X 6 ")	
1 Washington Iron "	
Logging camps tools & Roll ways	25000.00
Saw mill as it stands without the lumber on hand	500.00
McDaniels three acres more or less	$5.2200.00

We propose to sell you the above for $50000.00
you to pay us $38000.00 dollars in cash + twenty
four of the stock in your new company incorporated
at $50000.00 dollars. Above is given as an option
for 10 days from above date.

Cone Lumber Co
Geo W Cone
Pres

The original sale agreement for the Cone Lumber Co.

CHAPTER 3

The Early Days of Logging Above Black Rock

In all respects, Black Rock, Oregon was a classic logging town. Created by the railroad, it mushroomed as a hub of logging activity, then declined as logging and sawmilling operations moved on. At one time WVLCo. and three other companies had logging crews working out of Black Rock; three sawmills were located in the town.

By 1906 there were enough families in Black Rock to establish a post office, and Louis Gerlinger, Jr. was the first postmaster.

The area above Black Rock was the main source of timber for the WVLCo.'s Dallas mill for 33 years.

Black Rock took its name from a nearby outcropping of black shale rock on the Little Luckiamute River. At first there were only a few shacks in Black Rock, built along the edge of the railroad track. As the population grew, Black Rock took on the proportions of a self-sufficient community. There were two general merchandise stores, a saloon, boardinghouse, schoolhouse, barber shop, meat market and the red hall, a community center for social activities.

By 1910 Charles Spaulding, the lumberman-owner of the town, had platted a respectably-sized village with 22 blocks of lettered and numbered streets. Spaulding had planned for the town to be bone dry and genteel. Fortunately, the saloon keeper was never informed of it.

The population of Black Rock by 1910 was said to be about 600.

A typical day at Black Rock began well before dawn. Loggers with a lantern in one hand and a nose bag (lunchbox) in the other could be seen streaming down the railroad tracks. It took up to three hours to get to the logging site. Some workers were fallers who used the old misery whips (crosscut saws) to fall the stately firs. Others were high climbers who topped trees for spar trees (a tree with rigging used to haul logs from the cutting area to the loading area). Some worked on donkey engines. Up to four

19

engines could be needed to move logs from the place they were cut to the bed of the flatcar. Some workers cut wood to fuel the engines. As many as 75 men were employed in one logging operation (about three times today's requirement). The work was tough and exceedingly dangerous.

For the women and children of Black Rock, life was reasonably comfortable. The general store was well stocked. But "Ab" White, one of the Black Rock storekeepers, got his nickname because he seemed to be "Ab-solutely out" of whatever was most urgently needed. A call to Dallas would bring almost anything on the next train. A McKeen gasoline-powered rail passenger car took the ladies to Dallas for shopping. It was affectionately called "the skunk" because of its exhaust odor.

Saturday night was reserved for revelry, with the red hall the hub of social life. Townsfolk would enjoy magic lantern shows, roller skating, square dancing with local callers and musicians, box socials or wrestling. One of the most popular Saturday night entertainers was Nollie Dimmick. Nollie was a surveyor for the railroad who had a trained brown bear. He and the bear would wrestle, and betting was high on these occasions because sometimes Nollie would win.

The saloon was open late on Saturday night and old Red Connors would boil up big pots of chicken, given free to customers.

Black Rock had one very unusual monument to its credit. Fred Holman took over the duties of postmaster from Louis, Jr. Fred found an old Douglas fir stump about eight feet in diameter with a notch in it that once held a springboard (a board on which loggers would stand to fall a tree). He enlarged the notch a bit, smoothed it out, added an inkwell and built a post office around it.

The Holmans were Black Rock's aristocracy. They owned a house with papered walls and for years had the only bathtub in town. No one, not even the Holmans, had indoor plumbing.

The heyday of Black Rock was between 1910-1912. By 1913 one of the sawmills had pulled out and most of the companies working in the area had moved their men and families to logging camps above Black Rock. While it was to remain an important staging area for logging operations into the 1940's, it was a town doomed to die.

However, during 1926 Hollywood took notice of Black Rock. "The General", a civil war picture starring Buster Keaton, was filmed in Oregon with old locomotives refurbished in Dallas. A chase scene was shot above Black Rock. There was a huge 110-foot trestle at a switchback—the track went under the trestle, then switched back and went over it. In the film segment shot above Black Rock, one train was on top of the trestle being chased by another headed underneath. Actors threw fake railroad ties of canvas and chicken wire down on the track, "stopping" the train in pursuit.

II

WVLCo. had a series of five camps above Black Rock: Camp 2, Balderee Camp, Camp 18, K-Junction Camp and Boulder Camp. Each successive camp was further away from Black Rock into the mountains of the Coast Range. These camps were fairly typical of the thousands of logging camps in the mountains of the Pacific Northwest. The buildings were designed to fit on railroad flatcars for easy movement. Larger buildings like the cookhouse and commissary could be split to fit on two flatcars.

A typical camp would consist of some bunkhouses for eight men each, family houses, a cookhouse, schoolhouse, meat house, wash house and a commissary with the time-keeper's office. About 150 workers lived in a camp. Most lived in bunkhouses; family men had small cabins. Generally, the camps would be centrally located so they could remain stationary for several years while the area around them was logged.

There was little leisure time in the camps, but almost any night a logger could find some kind of activity at the commissary. U.S. currency was not used at camps. The Company had its own coinage—brass coins that loggers could draw from their pay to purchase candy, chewing tobacco and equipment from the Company store. Hefty card games with stacks of brass money were frequent, as were lotteries and punchboards. The commissary even had slot machines that took Company brass coins.

Liquor was not sold in the commissary, but beer was. However, it was possible to get liquor at the camps, even during Prohibition. During that dry period, a railroad brakeman named Donovan lived in an abandoned cookhouse at Camp 2. His attic was filled with corn, and occasionally he went into the woods, stoked up his copper still and made white lightning. Donovan would brew up a batch and place it in pint bottles, then put the bottles on ledges underneath the flatcars. In the morning when he went up to camp on the train, he'd give the numbers of the flatcars on which the moonshine was stashed to the timekeeper. After everyone left, the timekeeper would grab the hooch and sell it to the loggers for about $2 a pint. However, a logger could be fired for coming to work drunk.

Many of the men in the camps were foreigners—Swedes, Greeks and men from the Balkan States. Some couldn't read or write and many weren't U.S. citizens. Teachers at the camps often taught reading, writing and citizenship to adults as well as children. Many loggers acquired their naturalization papers while working at WVLCo. camps.

Accidents were common; many were serious. Sometimes more than once a week Dr. Starbuck, a Dallas physician retained by the Company, would be whisked off by speeder (a small gasoline-powered rail car) to Black Rock to attend to a serious injury.

Camps were generally closed in the winter when snowplows could no longer keep the tracks open.

III

WVLCo. camps had several colorful oddballs. One such fellow was Vinegar Bill. Vinegar Bill was a big, old Irishman and a highball locomotive engineer. Hot bearings on locomotives were always a problem, so he'd keep a gallon jug of vinegar in the cab to cool the bearings down. Most engineers just used water, but Bill was always in a hurry and vinegar cooled the bearings faster.

Bill didn't get out of camp much. And he didn't care for domestic chores. Every once in a while he'd send $20 to town for union suits (one-piece long underwear). He'd never wash his union suits—just wear them summer and winter until they smelled too strong, then burn them.

WVLCo. also had its share of legends. Bob Balderee was one. Bob came to WVLCo. as logging superintendent (super) just prior to the Great War. He turned a small logging outfit into an organized operation. He introduced highlead logging to the Company and organized the development of landings and railroad mainlines and spurs.

Gus Wiest was another legend. A big, brawny Swede with curly white hair, Gus had the ability to organize people. When he first came as super, crews were producing 20-30 carloads of logs daily. Within three or four months he had the men regularly loading 50-60 cars a day. When the mill needed logs desperately, crews could produce up to 100 carloads for Gus.

Wiest brought a variable-speed, interlocking Lidgerwood skidder to Black Rock. It could drag logs 2,000 feet, replacing cold decking and swinging. He became such an expert with the Lidgerwood that he was invited to give a paper explaining his use of the machine to the 1929 Pacific Logging Congress.

In 1930 Gus took on a trainee, Bill Swindells, a Portland civil engineer educated at Lehigh University, who had married George Gerlinger's middle daughter, Irene. After graduation, he had gone to work for the same company as his father, designing stores and display cases in Berkeley, California. In 1930 Gerlinger invited Swindells to try his hand at the lumber business and offered him the opportunity to buy an interest in WVLCo. Swindells began in the woods as a choker-setter (a person who fastens a cable device around a log so it can be hauled up for loading). For a time, he had his own logging operation called Swindells' Camp, as he learned the logging side of the business.

Eventually Gus Wiest moved on to his own gyppo (independently owned) logging operation. Swindells moved into logging management. Other men like Johnny Livingston, Art Wiley, Scuvie Schultz, Owen Doran, Walt Workman and Clergy McWhirter helped modernize logging above Black Rock.

As logging grew further and further away from Black Rock, the town became deserted. In 1939 the first truck logging was done on WVLCo. lands at Boulder Camp. Trucks hauled logs to camp, then loaded them onto rail cars for the trip to the mill. As the flexibility of trucks for log hauling became evident, more and more hauling was done by truck. In 1943 railroad logging above Black Rock ceased. For a time, Black Rock was used for truck maintenance and as a reload facility (to load logs from trucks onto Southern Pacific trains for the haul to Dallas).

Logging in the area wound down in the 1950's and Southern Pacific removed the last of the old Salem, Falls City and Western track from Black Rock to Dallas in 1961.

The railroad that had made Black Rock was itself finally laid to rest.

Today Black Rock isn't even a ghost town. Vigorous Douglas firs stand where children once played jacks and where Bill Ames' Dad used to sit on the porch and play the banjo and sing.

The fir stump used as a desk in the Post Office at Black Rock.

Davis and Sam Stevens pose with a 97-ton saddle tank American rod engine at Black Rock station.

The McKeen Gasoline Engine, affectionately known as "The Skunk", circa 1910.

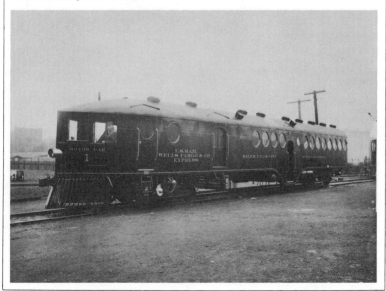

Camp 2 above Black Rock, a typical Willamette Valley Lumber Co. logging camp. Photo source: Harry Davis.

A donkey engine, used to move logs to railcars. Left to right: 1 and 2, the Dyer boys from Pedee, 3. unknown. 4. Cliff Burbank (who later became a Polk County Commissioner) 5. Charles King. Photo source: Cal Barnhart.

A typical logging operation above Black Rock. Photo source, Harry Davis. Railroad logging above Black Rock continued until 1943.

Willis Keller, sitting atop 160′ high spar tree.

The variable speed, interlocking Lidgerwood skidder.

CHAPTER 4

Efficiency Reigns: 1920 through the Great Depression.

By 1920 the Gerlingers and the Pittocks were sole owners of Willamette Valley Lumber Co.; Leadbetter having gone on to other lumber-related enterprises. H.L. Pittock had died, however, and his estate, with George Gerlinger as trustee, decided to sell its half interest in WVLCo.

WVLCo. had much to offer prospective owners. By 1920 it owned 11,006 acres of timberland containing over 334 million board feet of merchantable timber. Timber from another 10,000 acres under other ownerships was available and easily accessible. The plant facilities consisted of a sawmill with a 100,000 foot capacity on an eight hour shift, a planing mill with a capacity of 75,000 feet per day and dry kilns running at 35,000 feet daily. Net assets of the Company were valued at $1.5 million. Pittocks' half of the Company was offered at $375,000.

Gerlinger searched for other partners and soon found Orange M. Clark and his son, Wilson W. Clark. The Clarks had opened a sawmill in Linnton, Oregon (now Portland) the same year WVLCo. began. The Clark and Wilson Lumber Company was actually two mills on the same site—a typical steam-driven shotgun feed mill and a small log mill. It was a successful deep-water port mill that pioneered the Jap Square (a log squared on all four sides, then exported to Japan for further breakdown in Japanese mills).

While the Clarks held half interest in WVLCo. they remained silent partners, leaving the management of the Dallas mill to Gerlinger while they ran their own business. The Clarks later purchased a mill on the Columbia River at Prescott. (When they sold the Linnton mill in the mid-1940's it was the largest fir manufacturing plant in the state of Oregon.)

II

Another event in 1920 was not so fortunate. On July 10 a spectacular fire broke out at the Dallas sawmill, evidently caused by an overheated bearing on the slab conveyor. Wind whipped the flames to tremendous intensity, and only fast work by the plant's employees and Dallas citizenry saved the facility's finished lumber, two million feet of logs, the planing mill and box plant. The sawmill was a complete loss, but insurance covered the damage.

The work of rebuilding the sawmill began two days after the fire. The new mill, finished in January of 1921, was engineered by a well-known Portland sawmill designer. It had a capacity of 125,000 board feet on an eight hour shift.

Fire constantly plagued WVLCo. operations as it did all other lumber and logging companies. At times, mill and camp ownership seemed only a slightly better investment than a hand of poker. In 1922 a fire destroyed the mill's finished lumber inventory. In 1924 another dramatic fire burned the Company's logging camp, destroying with it the personal belongings of 140 loggers. Only two weeks later, a fire broke out at the mill burning the planer, dry kilns and some finished lumber. (The planer that burned was the one that had been saved during the 1920 fire. The loss was ironic in that an automatic sprinkler system for the planer had just arrived and had been scheduled for installation during the week following the fire.)

Each time portions of the mill were rebuilt, the Company improved them. The mill layout was redesigned for better efficiency. George Gerlinger and plant superintendents C.S. Keller and Erle Fulgham would spend hours discussing ideas for making the mill more productive and profitable. One way they thought they could increase profitability was using a tree shunned by most lumbermen—the hemlock.

About 1919 WVLCo. began developing specialty markets for hemlock. Hemlock is a softwood that grows under Douglas fir in the higher elevations of the Coast and Cascade Ranges. Hemlock wood is much wetter than fir and requires special handling. Hemlock lumber products must be dried to very exacting specifications. Many mills didn't have dry kilns in the 1920's and most of those that did, didn't want to bother with drying and marketing hemlock products. Because fir was plentiful, lumber companies left hemlock in the woods.

WVLCo.'s fee-owned (company owned) lands above Black Rock were about 70% Douglas fir, the remainder hemlock and minor amounts of other species. With that log mix, it was important to develop drying techniques and markets for hemlock.

WVLCo. cut hemlock into kiln-dried flooring, beveled siding, uppers (high quality materials used for doors, sashes and other exposed areas), molding, Jap baby squares and dimension lumber. The mill was one of two on the West Coast that could produce refrigerator stock (structural parts for refrigerators). Company salesmen worked to develop and maintain these specialty markets. At times the mill cut up to 60% hemlock.

Leftovers from the production of these products were sent to the box and lath mills. Lath was used as a backing for wall plaster and in making latticework. Hemlock was found to be an ideal wood for box-making as it wasn't resinous and did not impart a taste to the food it contained.

Any mill residues that couldn't be converted into a saleable product were sent to the boiler to make power. By the mid-1920's WVLCo. was producing power for its own needs by burning its wood waste. Surplus power was sold to Mt. States Power Company. Any leftover fiber beyond the capacity of the boiler went to the wigwam burner, a tepee-like structure used to burn waste wood and bark.

That wigwam burner became obsolete in 1927 when WVLCo. signed a contract to provide chips and hog fuel (waste wood for a boiler) for paper mills in Salem and Newberg.

Up until that time, paper mills bought whole hemlock logs or log blocks to break down into chips in the wood room of the paper mill. But WVLCo. offered chips ready for pulping when it installed the first commercial chipping operation on the West Coast.

In the beginning, workers picked bark-free scraps off conveyor belts and sent them to the chipper. Eventually, Company tinkerers invented slab-barkers—at first primitive rotary heads with knives, then water pressure barkers. These developments further increased the mill's fiber efficiency.

In 1929 WVLCo. tore down its wigwam burner. When a typical mill burned one-third of its leftovers from lumber processing in a wigwam burner, WVLCo. was selling or using everything. That policy helped the Company through the Great Depression.

III

In the late 1920's industry leaders realized there were too many mills with too much capacity on the West Coast. There was a great deal of talk about the advantages of forming a lumber cooperative in the Northwest. At the time, it was rumored that close to 100 companies had expressed an interest in forming a co-op to control production and prices.

It is not known whether WVLCo. considered participating in the Northwest co-op. But the Company did seriously consider joining in an amalgamation with several other Polk County mills to market the mills' products and provide for orderly shutdown of production in times of slack demand. There was also discussion of the amalgamation constructing a paper mill and converting facilities.

Because lumbermen of the day were a hardy, independent breed, few of the proposed co-ops were established. As a result, the lumber industry was left standing on the brink of the Depression with uncontrolled over-capacity.

WVLCo. put on two shifts in 1928, cutting about 260,000 board feet per day. It was the only mill in the area able to continue two 48-hour per week shifts throughout most of the Depression. Logging operations were going full bore; not a day was lost due to economic conditions.

Because the town's largest employer was working, the impact of the Depression on Dallas was less severe than on many other communities.

It was the mill's efficiency, ability to utilize fiber and resourceful marketing strategy that allowed WVLCo. to operate regularly during the Depression. The mill even made several equipment purchases in the early 1930's.

Times were not entirely good. Bill Swindells remembers watching Gerlinger sit down at the end of the month to decide which bills the Company could pay and which would have to wait until the next month. But Gerlinger was elated when he had to borrow money during the Depression for working capital and found his notes were the only ones in the industry the Federal Reserve would discount.

The mill closed only one time during the Depression, for lack of logs, as a result of a severe winter in the woods. "Thank goodness," Gerlinger told Swindells, "because we're losing so much money we should just as soon be shut down for a month." The Company had lumber sales of over $1 million in 1931 and made a slight profit.

Dallas and WVLCo. would have sailed through the Depression in a comparatively good position were it not for President Franklin D. Roosevelt's recovery program.

By 1933 lumbermen were still howling about controlling production and prices. One-third of the Douglas fir mills had closed their doors during the Depression. The remainder were barely eking by.

In 1933 the Roosevelt Administration's National Industrial Recovery Act was passed to try to stimulate employment in the private sector. Anti-trust laws were set aside and the government asked industries to get together to develop a plan for their own recovery. For the West Coast lumbermen, that wasn't difficult. They merely dusted off their old cooperative plans and set up the West Coast Lumbermen's Association as a bureau to set wages, prices and production quotas. Rules established by the Association became a part of the National Recovery Administration's Lumber Code.

The town of Dallas was actively involved in National Recovery programs. Grocers, garage and service station operators, and restaurant and lunch counter proprietors got together in their own groups, agreeing to provide new jobs.

Dallas was almost 100% subscribed to the NRA program when a crushing blow hit. The production quota given to the WVLCo. mill was for only one shift, 30 hours per week. The mill had been running two 48-hour shifts throughout the Depression. But in 1933 when recovery seemed at hand, it appeared the second shift would have to be dropped and the first shift abbreviated because of the Lumber Code.

Company management and townsfolk were stunned by the ruling. One hundred and fifty employees, with over 400 dependents, would have to be laid off from the mill. A like number would be laid off at the Company's Black Rock logging operations. Other mills were taking a 25% cut in hours; WVLCo. was being forced to suffer a 62½% cut.

The local Kiwanis Club immediately appointed a committee to request a hearing before the West Coast Lumbermen's Association.

At the hearing, Gerlinger presented a case for an exemption to the quota. He pointed out that close to half of the mill's production was specialty products not in competition with those of other mills. WVLCo. had a major contract to produce hemlock refrigerator stock for Norge and Kelvinator and was one of only two mills in the United States producing it. The mill also had contracts with a Chinese firm for making barrel staves and with an

English firm for wood blocks for parquet flooring. The mill had chip and hog fuel contracts with paper mills that could not be fulfilled if production were curtailed. WVLCo. provided a Salem paper mill with 40% of its hog fuel requirements and 35% of its chip needs. No other mill had facilities to meet their requirements.

The Company also had a contract to sell electricity to Mt. States Power that could not be fulfilled if the mill removed one shift. Gerlinger told the Association that the equivalent of one full shift was making products not in competition with other West Coast mills.

Management, employees and Dallas citizens were confident the quota would be modified because the West Coast Lumbermen's Association's committee on lumber production had the power to grant exceptions to production quotas. It was not modified. The ruling was appealed to the Board of Trustees of the WCLA. The Trustees upheld the ruling.

Gerlinger and several citizen and employee representatives went to Washington, D.C. to appeal the decision to the Lumber Code Authority, which had national responsibility for the Code. The decision was again upheld. An appeal was made to the National Recovery Administration. WVLCo. argued that past production should be a factor in Lumber Code quotas. Again, the decision was upheld. The Lumber Code compliance director told newspapers, "It unquestionably works a hardship on both labor and mill owners, but the recovery program was conceived on a long-term basis, and over-production must be eliminated first and will be for the best interests of the industry in the long run."

Townsfolk wrote to President Roosevelt himself. The President did not respond to the town's plea for help.

The West Coast Lumbermen's Association asked the Department of Justice to enforce the production quota. During all the appeals, the mill had continued to work two shifts. The West Coast Lumbermen's Association told WVLCo. management that the mill would have to close completely for two to four months because it had already exceeded production quotas. The Company also faced a $500 fine for each day it had violated the quota.

The town of Dallas was incredulous. The National Industrial Recovery Act, which was designed to create jobs, was about to put 300 loggers and sawmill workers on the street. The nation's recovery, it seemed, was to be harder on Dallas than the

Depression itself. In a scathing editorial, the editor of *The Polk County Itemizer-Observer* declared:

> In plain terms, the NRA administration has played directly into the hands of the timber moguls who have used its power and authority to stifle individual effort and to punish a timber operator who has been able to operate at a profit when they themselves have not. It has disregarded entirely the human equation of the employees and their families, who at the beginning of the winter will be thrown out of work and necessarily upon public charity—if there be enough public charity here to care for half the population of the community. The Willamette Valley Lumber Co. has been able to operate steadily and profitably during the past four or five years because Mr. Gerlinger has converted his waste products into saleable materials instead of carting them wholesale into a refuse burner and has developed new avenues of business . . . .

When Gerlinger returned from the National Recovery Administration hearing in Washington, D.C., he immediately filed for an injunction in federal district court to prevent the Justice Department's enforcement of the Lumber Code and to challenge the authority of the Code.

Gerlinger was granted the injunction on November 13, 1933, and the case was heard by Judge McNary in December. Mc-Camant, Thompson and King represented the Plaintiffs.

The case drew national attention. It was the first legal action challenging the Recovery Act in the Northwest. Wild stories were circulating nationwide, including a rumor that the Dallas townsfolk had ash-canned their blue eagle stickers (symbols of compliance with the Administration) in a madly unpatriotic act.

At the hearing, Gerlinger told the court that tests had been conducted which showed the mill would have to work a minimum of 48 hours a week to meet its hog fuel, chip and power obligations.

Late in January 1934 the district court lifted the injunction and ruled WVLCo. would have to comply with production and 30-hour shift quotas. However, McNary questioned the Code's authority to inflict penalties on the Dallas mill and he continued the order restraining enforcement. He said the mill would not have to close to make up for past violations of production quotas or incur a fine. It would be sufficient to lay off one shift immediately.

About 250 sawmill workers and loggers were laid off. Effort was made to keep employees with the most seniority and the most dependents. However, workers with up to 16 years' seniority were laid off. A new employee with 10 dependents had to be released from the payroll.

WVLCo. decided not to appeal the decision. It had other plans. During the course of his many appeals, Gerlinger had become intimately familiar with the Lumber Code. He'd discovered that while the Code could prevent his operating a second shift at the Dallas mill, it could neither prevent construction of a new mill nor deny the new mill a quota. It was about time, Gerlinger decided, for the Dallas mill to build a compact little mill for processing small logs. A week after the federal court judge delivered his decision, Gerlinger announced in the local newspaper the arrival of equipment for a new small log mill planned for start-up in one month, with a 10,000 board foot per hour capacity. Of course, more men would be hired to run the mill and provide the logs. Dallas shared Gerlinger's smugness. The new mill was called Mill G after Colonel Greeley, secretary of the West Coast Lumbermen's Association.

Gerlinger continued to oppose the Code. Later in 1934 he headed a group of sawmill owners laying plans to oppose the price-fixing features of the Code.

Less than a year later in June 1935 the U.S. Supreme Court declared certain key phases of the National Industrial Recovery Act invalid, abolishing the Lumber Code.

Orange M. Clark

The 1920 fire, Willamette Valley Lumber Co.

George Gerlinger

Wilson W. Clark

CHAPTER 5

The Acquisition of Corvallis Lumber Company
and the Snow Peak Timberlands

For many years, WVLCo. had been connected with the Corvallis Lumber Co. through half ownership of Corvallis Logging, which furnished logs to Corvallis Lumber. The Corvallis mill was extremely inefficient, and two consecutive sets of owners failed to make it profitable. The mill was closed throughout most of the Depression. In January 1935 George Gerlinger bought the mill and named Bill Swindells manager. George Young stayed on as mill superintendent.

The mill was no prize. It was an old belt-driven sawmill producing only about 50-60,000 board feet per day.

Gerlinger and Swindells gradually improved or replaced the mill's equipment. The headrig, which had been two circle saws, was replaced by a band. A gang saw was installed and all of the machinery was converted to electric drive when a hog fuel boiler and electric turbines were added.

Lumber was sold through the Dallas sales office, although Corvallis Lumber was kept a separate entity from WVLCo.

Manufacturing costs were reduced, efficiency was improved and the operation began to show a profit.

Now there were two mouths to feed; two hungry mills requiring a daily ration of logs. WVLCo. had purchased Coast Range timberlands as it could. But it was not enough. In 1923 the Company bought its first stumpage from the federal government. WVLCo. and Corvallis Lumber Co. lands were interspersed with Oregon and California (O&C) Railroad grant lands. These lands had been given to the Oregon and California Railway by the government as an incentive to complete a proposed railroad. The government took the lands back after terms of the contract were violated and began to offer stumpage for sale. Purchases from these O&C lands plus open market timber purchases had supplemented the Company's fee timber base above Black Rock since 1923.

II

George Gerlinger had a clear perspective of the problems facing Oregon's lumber industry. In 1919 Governor Ben Olcott had appointed Gerlinger to the Oregon State Board of Forestry. He served on the board for 29 years—longer than any other lumberman.

At first the Board, which ran the state's Department of Forestry, was interested only in fire protection. Soon it began to preach fire prevention. From there, the Board took the quantum leap to a variety of concerns about Oregon's forestry future.

Gerlinger was instrumental in establishing "A Forest Policy for Oregon" which was approved by the Board in 1920. It was a comprehensive twenty-point program outlining ideal standards for management of federal, state and private forest lands. It spoke of the need to protect forest lands from fire, insects and disease; called for the development of nurseries to provide seedlings for reforestation; and pointed to the need for some kind of tax incentives to allow private landowners to keep their cutover lands.

Taxes on cutover lands had been a particular problem for landowners. Many, unable to pay taxes on unproductive land, had allowed their property to revert to the counties. WVLCo. had kept most of its cutover land but was itself feeling the tax pinch.

In 1929 Gerlinger was instrumental in encouraging the State Legislature to pass the Reforestation Act, which established a small annual tax on each acre and a yield tax at the time of harvest. The minimal annual tax allowed owners to keep their properties without being burdened by heavy taxes on non-productive land. At harvest time, the landowner paid a fairly heavy yield tax, paying back the taxing district for minimum payments throughout the years. Probably more than anything else, this Act helped companies and individuals retain cutover properties.

Gerlinger felt an urgency to adopt practices to maintain the productivity of Oregon's forests. In the 27th annual report of the State Board of Forestry (1937), Gerlinger wrote:

> Our operators recognize that their future and that of their employees is closely bound to the wise use of the forest lands of the state. For that reason, the industry has supported the enactment of sound practical laws relating to the forest problems of Ore-

gon, and in addition, it works under rules of forest practice formulated by the industry that go beyond the state laws in an effort to maintain the productivity of forest lands. These forest practice rules are a recognition of an obligation by the industry itself and those dependent on it toward permanent forest for the state.

Gerlinger was also active in encouraging management of O&C Administration lands. For years, the O&C Administration had given these lands away to homesteaders and had sold some timber. The O&C Administration's critics, and there were many of them, felt its land management policies fell somewhere between lackadaisical and criminal.

Congress approved the Sustained Yield Act in 1937, which directed the O&C Administration to manage its lands to provide a sustained yield of timber in perpetuity. The method of providing for sustained yield was through an annual allowable cut and careful maintenance of a second-growth forest. Some Oregon timbermen balked at the idea of a cutting limit on these lands and claimed that sustained yield would not work in Douglas fir forests. Gerlinger chided these obstructionists by publicly stating that the O&C proposals were merely extensions of methods that responsible timbermen had long employed.

Because of his vision and support, Gerlinger was named to the first Board of Advisors to the O&C Administration, a citizens' group that helped set policy for the agency.

III

Because of his deep involvement with the Board of Forestry and the O&C Administration, Gerlinger had a clear picture of the state's timber supply future. That heightened his awareness of his own companies' timber supply problems. By 1938 WVLCo.'s holdings consisted of two categories: Old growth ready for harvest and young stands under 30 years of age. There was only enough old growth to last five or six more years. Corvallis Lumber was in a similar position.

Gerlinger was reluctant to see his company dependent upon the public timber market. Yet, there were few large tracts of old growth timber in the Coast Range available for purchase. The only suitable stands of old growth were in the less accessible Cascade Mountain Range across the Willamette Valley from Dallas and Corvallis.

In 1938 WVLCo. purchased 9,745 acres in eastern Linn County (in the Cascade Range) from the Hammond Lumber Company. In 1939 another 3,880 acres in the same area were purchased from Wright-Blodgett.

The Company bought only a portion of the timberland available for sale. In retrospect, it would have been wise to purchase the entire tract. But economic conditions in the timber industry were still unsettled and management thought it unwise to take risks by buying excessive amounts of timberland. In addition, funds for the purchase of such lands were not available.

The logistics of getting the logs to Dallas might have discouraged lesser men, but the operation provided a stimulating challenge for Gerlinger, Swindells and their new engineer, Aaron Mercer. Snow Peak Camp, named for Snow Peak, a sharp projectile mountain rising to the north of the area to be logged, was built 15 miles away from the nearest railroad crossing at Griggs, some 65 miles from Dallas. It was, by those days' standards, an unusually long haul.

But the trio were creative thinkers, and the distance challenge stimulated a revolutionary solution.

Truck hauling was not new in 1939. For years loggers had been phasing out railroad logging in favor of truck hauling. The trio was convinced that Snow Peak should be an all-truck operation using a new twist—a private mainline haul road.

Other logging companies were using public roads to get their logs out. The Snow Peak Logging Company was the first to build a private mainline logging road as a substitute for using existing public roads. The road went from the timber at Snow Peak to a holding pond and rail transfer site at Griggs.

The private road allowed the Company to use oversized trucks not permitted on public roads and to avoid road taxes. The custom-built Kenworth trucks introduced at Snow Peak were so large, they could not be operated on public roads even when empty. When fully loaded, these monsters would literally push the roadbed into the surrounding fields. One record load out of Snow Peak contained 24,761 board feet net.

The private mainline wasn't the only innovation the trio had up their sleeves for Snow Peak. Prior to this time, logging had followed a typical pattern: A railroad line was put into a valley, the area was logged clean, then the rails were moved to the next valley. When trucks began to replace the old iron horses, logging continued in the same pattern.

WVLCo. management initiated a whole new concept of logging at Snow Peak called the staggered setting system. A system of mainline and spur roads was constructed in the Snow Peak timberlands. Instead of logging everything the road touched, a checkerboard pattern of logging commenced. Fire prevention and prompt reforestation were the principal benefits of this system. Leaving green timber between clearcuts resulted in smaller accumulations of slash and thus, less fire hazard. The system also left a seed source for reforestation.

A side benefit of the staggered setting system was almost year-round logging. The Company could log at high elevations in the summer and move to lower elevations in the winter and spring when weather closed the high country.

The system was extended to the Company's Black Rock and Corvallis operations. The merits of this logging system were quickly recognized and adopted by public and private landowners all over the Northwest. The staggered setting system was uniquely adaptable to first-cycle cutting in large, old-growth Douglas fir stands.

Willamette Valley's logging trucks were so large and heavy they were unable to operate on public roads even when empty.

CHAPTER 6

World War II Production; The Labor Movement

A brisk, chilly wind swept through the yard at the Willamette Valley Lumber Co. as the night shift came on duty the evening of October 10, 1940. The men at the planer mill wore warmer clothing than usual and talked about whether the winter would be a tough one.

Simultaneously, the 25 men on the planer crew broke their easy working stride to look up in horror. "Fire!" the men shouted, almost in unison, dropping their work to head for fire hoses in the yard.

The men broke out hose but were soon driven back by the heat of the fire. By the time the alarm sounded, flames were already leaping skyward, the blaze spreading with an ever-increasing roar. Dallas Fire Department volunteers arrived with three pumpers and an auxilliary truck. Employees from other shifts and townsfolk came to gawk and pitch in. Little could be done. Wind spread the flames rapidly into the drying sheds, shipping sheds and the planer mill. The fire burned so intensely it created almost cyclonic winds, whipping flame and ash high into the sky beyond hope of control. The fire was so hot it welded the wheels of boxcars to the railroad track.

Firefighters from Salem, Monmouth, Independence, Sheridan, Falls City and Willamina arrived at the scene to help local firefighters. They could only wet down the roofs of buildings not yet consumed. Yard employees drove lumber carriers in and out of the flames and smoke trying to save as much finished lumber as possible. Volunteers worked all through the night. Many were drenched to the skin; others had the shirts burned off their backs.

The flames could be seen for some 20 miles. Ducks, confused by the false dawn created by the fire, circled over the mill, many trying to land in the smoke, mistaking it for fog above a lake.

Bill Swindells was at a lumbermen's meeting in Victoria, British Columbia the night of the fire. He'd received a call from Dallas rather late and returned to his room in the Empress Hotel with several friends to wait for the operator to put the call through.

He and his friends were sitting on the twin beds in the room when suddenly the chandelier hanging between the two beds crashed to the floor. Staring at the smashed chandelier, Swindells exclaimed, "My God, the mill has burned!" Only a few minutes later the confirming phone call came.

At dawn, exhausted firefighters surveyed the wreckage. The buildings on the south and west—the sawmill, dry kilns and power plant—were saved by wind direction. But the planer, drying sheds, shipping sheds, 10 million feet of the best lumber in the yard (including 2 million feet of aircraft lumber), a dozen box cars and a new cut-up plant (ready for installation of machinery) were all destroyed. Some lumber was saved, but it was mostly the poorer grades. The damage was estimated at over $500,000 and only a portion of the loss was covered by insurance. It was truly the worst fire in Dallas' history.

Disbelief at the magnitude of the fire soon gave way to an unsettling fear. Sawmill equipment was exceedingly scarce because of the military build-up. The uninsured loss had been substantial. Some of the townsfolk wondered if the mill would be rebuilt.

Then, without fanfare, Swindells began building a new family home in Dallas, and 100 men were signed up to begin construction of new mill buildings while awaiting arrival of equipment. The other 200 workers were placed temporarily in jobs with other mills.

II

By the time the mill was ready for start-up in February 1941 World War II was well underway in Europe.

Willamette Valley Lumber Co. had become well-known for its production of aircraft lumber after the early days of World War I. During the war, the United States and its allies had used spruce exclusively for the propeller and the most strategic parts of airplanes. The British had subsequently discovered the qualities of noble fir. When the British came to the United States to discuss manufacture of aircraft stock, they chose the WVLCo. office in Dallas as the location to meet with producers to discuss lumber specifications.

After Pearl Harbor, the Corvallis and Dallas mills both produced lumber for the war effort. Some of the lumber was for rebuilding bridges and docks, but the most difficult challenge was the production of aircraft stock, most of which was noble fir. Recovery of aircraft stock ran about 10 percent. In other words, if a shipment of 10,000 feet were required by the War Department, 100,000 feet of logs would have to be cut. Unfortunately, noble fir grew in small pockets at high altitudes closed to loggers in the winter months by snow. A stockpile of logs had to be cut during the summer months by an ever-dwindling number of loggers.

Because of the priority placed on noble fir aircraft stock, logging was done selectively. Snow Peak crews would push in a road, often under adverse weather conditions, then loggers would take out only noble fir trees, leaving the vast majority of the stand, Douglas fir and hemlock, for later.

WVLCo. had a special mill for the breakdown of aircraft lumber. Logs would be cut on two sides on the headrig at the big mill. If they were quality logs—sound, clear, straight and fine-grained—they would be sent to the aircraft sawmill for further breakdown.

The mill produced nearly 4.4 million board feet of aircraft stock in 1943.

On September 21, 1943, the Army recognized WVLCo.'s contribution to the war effort by presenting it the coveted Army-Navy E Award for excellence in production for the war effort.

The award ceremony was witnessed by a crowd of several hundred employees, their families, townsfolk and visitors. Businesses were closed for the program and flags were displayed on downtown Dallas streets. A military band from nearby Camp Adair played martial music while Colonel Sherrill from Washington, D.C. presented the mill with a special "E" award pennant to fly from the flagpole. Each of the employees was decorated with the E pennant lapel pin for his part in the production of high-quality lumber.

In addition to working overtime to produce lumber for the war effort, the men at the mills received numerous awards for their participation in war bond and blood bank drives. The Dallas mill served as a scrap metal collection center for Polk County.

In March 1944 the Dallas mill was awarded a second Army-Navy E Award for "meritorious services on the production front". A new pennant flew over the mill—this one with a white star.

III

The war provided the impetus for much needed salvage. The tremendous demand for lumber created by the war made it possible to log snags (fire-killed trees) on WVLCo. lands. Some of these snags had been standing for more than 20 years, and recovery from them was about 40 percent of the estimated volume before the fire.

In ordinary times, recovery wouldn't have paid, but the war made salvage very desirable. A tremendous fire danger was removed with very little damage to the young growth beneath and fiber for the war effort was saved.

Manpower during this era was scarce. There was no Spruce Division in World War II as there had been in World War I. But an invention came along that helped increase the production of the available workforce—the power saw. WVLCo. went to Vancouver, B.C. to a Stihl distributor and brought the first power saws into Oregon.

IV

Gerlinger and WVLCo. employees had been extremely active in the Loyal Legion of Loggers and Lumbermen (4L's) during World War I and for several years thereafter. During the Depression they didn't need a bargaining unit, so the 4L's died a death of disinterest.

Company management always tried to be fair with employees. In 1929 the mill introduced group life and health insurance through Aetna, with the Company and the employee sharing the premiums. The Company tried, even during the Depression, to provide its employees a reasonable wage.

In 1935 lockouts and strikes in Columbia River tidewater mills halted production there for several weeks. Not only were the unions fighting to unionize workers, the AFL and the CIO were fighting each other for representation.

In May of 1935 the Black Rock logging operations were closed by management for several days when it became apparent there were enough agitators at Black Rock to cause trouble if an attempt were made to continue operating. The Dallas mill kept working, but the men were uneasy. Unrepresented by any union, they were a prime target for organization.

In 1936 the 4L's was reorganized at the Dallas mill to forestall attempts by the AFL to organize. About 375 of the mill's eligible employees voted for the 4L's as their bargaining agent.

However, the Wagner Act of 1937 banned unions in which employers and employees jointly participated. Gerlinger and two other lumbermen joined in encouraging the formation of a regional, all-employee union, called the Industrial Employees Union (IEU). The purpose of the IEU was to promote collective bargaining, maintain wage and hour schedules and insure a uniform industry wage scale. At Dallas, IEU received 238 votes, the AFL, 31; the CIO, 9; and the concept of a private employees' union was supported by 22. IEU Local No. 35 was formed.

Tensions remained high. Mill workers still were afraid of violence from larger unions.

Early in 1941 the National Labor Relations Board (NLRB) dissolved Local No. 35 and set up a new election for union representation. This time employees asked for the IEU by a two-thirds vote.

In May 1941 the NLRB refused to recognize the IEU as a bargaining unit.

Again an election was set up. This time 280 out of 300 eligible workers brought in the AFL, forming Local No. 2714. But the CIO, disputing which union actually won, asked for another election. The NLRB granted the re-election but the results were much the same.

In May of 1944 the Dallas AFL members followed the lead of other lumber company employees and walked out for six days in protest against the National War Labor Board's refusal to grant lumber workers a pay increase. Corvallis mill employees continued to work.

Both the union and the Company referred to the Dallas strike as a "piscatorial incident"—a six-day fishing break. The union was not striking as a result of a dispute with management. Nonetheless, the Company, in a letter to employees published in the local paper, called the incident "a new and unfamiliar milestone". Further, management stated, "It is a source of some satisfaction on all sides that this particular delay in production at Dallas has not arisen from any direct conflict between you and ourselves. In that regard, the long record remains unbroken."

But it was, indeed, an unfamiliar milestone—the first strike in the Company's 38-year history.

*The E-Award Pennant is raised above the Willamette
Valley Lumber Co., September 21, 1943.*

George Gerlinger receives the Army-Navy E Award for meritorious achievement on the production front from Col. Sherrill, as most of the town of Dallas watches.

Aircraft lumber being produced at the Corvallis mill.

CHAPTER 7

The 1945 Fire and Experiments with Reforestation

Considering its Northern latitude, western Oregon has an exceptionally mild climate. Winters are rainy with only occasional flurries of snow. Summers are rainy but interrupted with extended periods of warm weather. Occasionally summer will bring extremely hot, dry weather, accompanied by warm east winds. Summer tourists consider the weather pleasant. But it's enough to raise the hackles on the back of an Oregon logger's neck. That's forest fire weather.

The sun bakes fuels on the forest floor and the east wind sucks out the last dregs of moisture. Under such conditions, campfires thought to be extinguished two months previously can spring into life, consuming a forest. A cigarette butt crushed against a stump can be the source of a holocaust.

Such conditions existed during July of 1945. For several days the daytime temperature hovered over 90 degrees. When the weather broke on the 14th, everyone heaved a sigh of relief.

But about 1:30 on the afternoon of Monday the 16th, a puff of smoke was seen on the horizon west of Dallas. By evening the fire had spread to 100 acres of WVLCo. lands. Firefighters had circled the blaze with fuel-less trails by Tuesday afternoon and had some hope of controlling it. But high winds fanned the flames again, causing them to jump the fire lines. The winds carried embers that ignited another blaze a half mile away early Wednesday morning. The small blaze spread quickly, joining with the main fire.

Spot fires were numerous, but firefighters had to ignore them. By Thursday afternoon the fire had grown to 2,800 acres. A wind shift brought ash and smoke into Dallas, dirtying laundry and obscuring the sun. The small log mill was closed, releasing plant workers to join the 125 loggers and state firefighters already on the fire lines.

On Friday morning, firefighters had the blaze two-thirds circled and were again hopeful of control. But once more the fire raged out of control, nearly trapping a group of firefighters. New gains forced the over 300 firefighters back time and again from their fire trails. WVLCo.'s old logging camp and about 3 million feet of logs at the camp were destroyed. By nightfall of its worst day yet, the fire had consumed a total of 6,000 acres, and plans were being made to evacuate the small town of Pioneer, west of Dallas. Dallas officials expressed concern as the fire raged within two miles of the town's water supply intake.

A welcome rain greeted firefighters Saturday morning, temporarily quieting the Polk County fire and another large one to the north in the area known as the "Tillamook Burn".

The rains and rising humidity were not enough to quench the flames. By Sunday the fire had consumed 8,000 acres. About 500 black soldiers from Fort Lewis, Washington were sent to man the fire lines.

The blaze had been burning mostly in logged-over lands. But by Tuesday morning, eight days after the fire started, flames reached a recently logged area, burning over 10 million feet of felled and bucked timber. Logging crews worked desperately to hold the fire back from a new WVLCo. logging camp. Flames licked within 200 feet of the buildings as men on bulldozers circled the camp with wide fire trails. The fire finally swept by, leaving the camp untouched.

The large sawmill was closed and men were sent to join the fire crews. A strange sight greeted the 900 firefighters on the line at dawn on Wednesday morning—a dense, dripping fog. That evening after flying over the fire line, State Forester Nels Rogers announced that the fire was pretty well under control, but that the area would remain a danger zone for the rest of the summer.

All the next day crews worked at mopping up the hot spots, falling snags, completing fire trails and patrolling the fire perimeter. A week later, after building over 50 miles of fire line, the soldiers were released to fight the fire in the Tillamook Burn. About 25 conscientious objectors from a camp near Elkton, Oregon arrived to help logging crews mop up. Mill crews returned to make up for lost production.

But Nature had no respect for the war effort. On August 18 east winds again fanned the remaining embers, causing a phenomenon that strikes terror in the hearts of fire crews—a crown fire. (Instead of burning on the ground, a crown fire burns through the tops of trees. Virtually nothing can stop it.) The crown fire terrorized firefighters for over four hours, consuming over 700 acres of green timber. Only cooler weather, a shift in the wind direction and finally, rain, allowed the firefighters to control the blaze. The mop up was a slow process. Parts of the fire were over four miles from the nearest road and pack horses had to be used to get tools and supplies to fire crews.

When the flames were finally doused by the fall and winter rains, officials surveyed the wreckage. Some 13,000 acres had burned on WVLCo. and O&C Administration lands, including 100 million feet of green timber, 12 million board feet of felled and bucked logs and an old camp.

II

Today reforestation of a burn like the '45 fire would be immediate and automatic. As soon as weather allowed, crews would be combing the hills with their hoedads, planting a new crop.

But reforestation was no sure bet in 1945. In fact, foresters were only beginning to experiment with different methods of restocking burned and cutover lands. However, the need for reforestation had been recognized for many years.

In 1940 Gerlinger and the other members of the Oregon State Board of Forestry were responsible for writing and lobbying the legislature for passage of Oregon's Conservation Act. The Act required loggers to harvest in a manner that would insure a new crop of trees. It provided ground rules for the protection and perpetuation of commercial forest lands. Stewart Holbrook, logger-turned-writer, described the new Act to the nation in the *New York Herald Tribune.*

> This law is not just another attempted crackdown by government on the lumber industry, which often, and many times unjustly, has served as a whipping boy for federal administrations since 1933. The law was written, proposed and fostered by Oregon loggers and lumbermen themselves, working closely with ranching and agricultural interests. Basically, it is an attempt by thoughtful lumbermen to control the irresponsible minority of their fellows of the old fashioned

cut-out-and-get-out school. It is a practical law, based not on esthetic theory but on long experience.

During the next year, industry followed up with its own method of promoting good forestry—The American Tree Farm System. While the tree farm system was a public relations tool designed to convince an increasingly concerned public that something was being done to manage forest lands, it was more than just a gimmick. Forest land owners signed an agreement to manage their lands as tree farms—perpetual producers of wood fiber. In addition, they agreed to protect the lands from fire, insects and disease and to harvest in such a manner as to insure a new crop of trees. To maintain their tree farm status, owners in the Douglas fir region were required to submit records to the organization known today as the Industrial Forestry Association to show they had met their commitment to forest management. Tree farms were periodically inspected as well.

Weyerhaeuser's Clemons Tree Farm in Washington was the first "tree farm" in the U.S. In 1943 the Black Rock and Snow Peak Tree Farms (renamed the George T. Gerlinger Tree Farm and the Wilson W. Clark Tree Farm in July of 1968) were inducted into the system as a part of a second large group of tree farms.

III

While there had been plenty of burns in Oregon larger than the 1945 fire, little had been done to rehabilitate fire-scorched lands. The increasing awareness of the need to reforest, whether after a natural disaster or a man-made clearcut, brought the WVL Co. and O&C foresters together in the fall of 1945 to discuss rehabilitation of the fire area.

The fire had left unburned islands of live trees in some areas. These, coupled with perimeter trees, would provide an adequate source to seed naturally the majority of the 13,000 acres burned, the foresters felt. But 5,200 acres would need some reforestation assistance from man.

Since little was known about successful reforestation, foresters from both landowners decided to use the 5,200 acres as a giant reforestation testing plot. They agreed to try different methods of seeding, then monitor the results to determine the best techniques.

In January of 1946, 800 acres were seeded from an airplane. The next year numerous trial plots were established. Some were seeded with a hand-cranked seeder, some with a "gun" which shot seeds into the ground and some received seeding with both methods. Port Orford cedar, Sitka spruce, Western red cedar and hemlock were used in addition to Douglas fir at different elevations and sun exposures. Some spots were laced with poison two weeks prior to seeding to control rodents.

Reforestation efforts continued into the 1950's, sometimes using helicopters, sometimes hand-planting seedlings. The experiment was a success, but the forest wasn't. A multitude of lessons were learned, however. One entire planting of Port Orford cedar in a valley failed completely because aerial seeding was done on crusty snow. When the seeds hit the snow, they rolled down into the creek at the bottom of the valley. A planting of ponderosa pine failed, teaching foresters another valuable lesson: Reforestation is most successful when native stock is used. Foresters also found through this and other experiments that reforestation by airplane, hand-crank seeder or gun just wasn't successful. Aerial seeding provided very poor seed distribution. The experiment proved the only truly successful method to reforest Douglas fir was with hand planting of seedlings. It was years before the '45 burn was successfully reforested.

IV

It was the last major fire on Company lands. The state of Oregon began to place fire prevention restrictions on logging operations, requiring fire fighting equipment at logging sites and shutting down operations during periods of extreme fire hazard. WVLCo., however, developed its own fire policies which were much stricter than those of the State. Obsolete logging trucks were converted to fire fighting equipment. Fire caches, filled with hose and fire fighting tools, were established in several locations on Company tree farms. Weather stations were built and fire wardens continually checked air temperature, winds and humidity during fire season. Fuel moisture sticks were placed throughout the tree farms to gauge the dryness of the fuels on the forest floor.

One other major continuing program was begun as a fire prevention measure: Snag removal. Snags (fire-killed trees) attract lightning and their punky, rotten insides throw long-burning embers that are carried great distances by the wind. The only way to remove the fire hazard was to cut the snags down. There was no economically usable wood in most snags, so loggers would cut the snags and leave them lay, allowing them to break down in the soil to provide nutrients for the new crop of trees.

Thousands of snags were felled in the 50's in the Black Rock 1945 fire area. A snag-free corridor seven miles long and one-half mile wide was established along the Black Rock mainline road. Over 20,000 snags were felled in the old Crabtree Burn and 20,000 in other areas on the Snow Peak Tree Farm. Another 18,000 snags were cleared from 450 acres of Company lands on Old Blue Mountain out of Corvallis, at the nagging of OSU forestry professor T. J. Starker. These programs prevented a repetition of catastrophes like the 1945 Black Rock fire.

Bill Hagenstein, executive director of the Industrial Forestry Association, presents a tree farm certificate to Bill Swindells on the twenty-fifth anniversary of the American Tree Farm System. Willamette was among a second, large group of landowners to join the tree farm system after the Clemmons Tree Farm.

The aftermath of the 1945 fire.

Fire protection during the 1950's was aided by many new-fangled devices like the portable radio (Foster woods superintendent Walt Workman), permanent weather stations (Sam Smith, assistant forester and chief fire warden), fire trucks and tool caches.

Reforestation by seeding from the air was proven un-satisfactory by experimentation in the 1945 burn. Hand planting of seedlings proved to be the only reliable method of insuring reforestation.

The Hill Contract and the Construction of Willamette National Lumber Co.

"In 1939, I could see that we were running out of timber and I could see Corvallis with practically no timber at all. I was nervous about a job," Bill Swindells says.

Even after the Hammond and Wright-Blodgett timber purchases, the long-term fee timber supply outlook was bleak. In fact, Bill Swindells, Jr. remembers his Grandfather Gerlinger telling him that if he were interested in a career in the timber industry, he'd most likely have to pursue that interest in Brazil.

But in 1943 WVLCo. management began negotiations to obtain adequate timber supply for expansion. Bill Swindells approached Dave Mason, a well-known timber consultant and advisor to the Hill family, about a long-term timber supply contract on Hill lands.

The Hill family, of the "railroad" Hills in St. Paul, Minnesota owned a substantial amount of timberland near Sweet Home, Oregon, some 20 miles southeast of Snow Peak. The land had never been touched until about 1940 when the Hill interests contracted with McDowell Creek Logging of Sweet Home to log a small portion of their timberland to start a sheep ranch.

Swindells proposed to build a sawmill in the Sweet Home area to process logs from Hill lands, and in return, pay the Hills a percentage of the mill's gross profit.

Swindells and Mason had several discussions before taking the matter to the Hills in St. Paul. The Hill lands contained a fair amount of hemlock, a material WVLCo. had learned to use profitably. It seemed a natural marriage. Early in 1946 a fifteen-year contract for 1 billion feet of timber was signed that guaranteed the Hills a percentage of the gross profit of the mill or a minimum stumpage price, whichever was greater.

In February of 1946 incorporation papers were filed for Willamette National Lumber Co., a corporation separate from Willamette Valley Lumber Co. Wilson Clark was president of the new corporation; George Gerlinger, vice president; Bill Swindells, secretary; and Maurie Clark (Wilson's son), treasurer.

Sid Lewis, manager of the Dallas sawmill, was named general manager of both operations. Paul Morgan, with a long and varied experience in sawmill management, joined Willamette National as resident manager.

Because of the need for more sophisticated cost control and accounting procedures as a result of the Hill contract, A. R. Morgans was hired as an accountant. With 21 years' experience as an accountant with the West Coast Lumbermen's Association, Morgans was well-qualified to manage the increasingly complicated financial affairs of the related enterprises.

Engineers Aaron Mercer, Dutch LeFors and Rex Pemberton searched the Sweet Home area for a site for the new mill. They finally settled on a piece of ground in an area known as Foster, about three miles east of Sweet Home.

With management in place and a site selected, there was only one further problem—equipment. New sawmill machinery was impossible to secure because of pent-up demand from the war. The mill had to settle for used equipment. Maintenance men were hired to completely recondition most of the motors. A blacksmith fabricated needed parts. Even old electrical conduit was used in the mill because new materials were unavailable.

Willamette National Lumber Co., named because of its proximity to the Willamette National Forest, opened on May 23, 1947. The mill's annual capacity was 70 million board feet on two shifts. In addition to the sawmill, the mill had a planing mill, dry kilns, a 60-acre log storage pond, shipping shed, machine shed and a retail building materials store. A powerhouse was installed at the site capable of producing all the power needed to run the mill plus extra to sell to Mt. States Power.

Willamette National had cost $2.5 million to construct —three times original estimates. It was not all that profitable at first. Even before the mill opened, the Corvallis Lumber Company was merged into Willamette National and for many months the profits of the Corvallis mill kept the new corporation afloat.

II

From the outset, labor was a problem. Housing for families was at a premium, so it was difficult to attract stable family men. The Company brought a cookhouse and bunkhouses from Snow Peak Camp down to Foster to provide some housing for single men in a camp they called Foster Lodge. Willamette National built a handful of houses for married men. Other homes were rented by the Company, then subleased to workers at a reasonable price, usually less than the original rental. There were not enough homes to go around, forcing some newcomers to live in tents.

The mill and woods operations were ripe for labor problems. And they came soon. Woods operations experienced a series of "stump strikes". The crew would go to the woods and if they didn't like the day's work or the way the bullbuck spit, they'd just sit down on stumps and wait until a company "official" came to settle the difference.

In mid-1948 a labor dispute took both the mill and the woods operations out. The CIO struck over three men—the cook, the power saw mechanic and the high climber. The head cook at the cookhouse, they claimed, was an ornery SOB who served unpalatable food and swore at the kitchen help (he was also a member of the AFL). The powersaw mechanic and the high climber, they claimed, deserved more pay. So the union took the boys out. The Company considered the strike frivolous and refused to meet with union leaders until they promised to get serious about negotiation. The Sweet Home weekly newspaper, the *New Era,* did a booming business as both sides talked to each other through paid advertisements. After 17 days a compromise was offered and the crews went back to work. But labor problems of a similar nature continued to plague the mill for years afterward. Because of the labor unrest at Willamette National, Ralph Boone was hired as the Company's first full time industrial relations manager.

In order to attract a stable work force, Willamette National began to offer a liberal payroll deduction plan for home construction. An employee who purchased a lot could go to the mill's retail outlet and buy all his building materials on credit. A small amount was deducted from his paycheck weekly until the bill for the house was paid.

The mill did a lot to help stabilize the community. Dances were held, civic projects undertaken and a Company magazine, the *Willamette Echo,* was published. The *Echo* featured family news, photos of children and snapshots of houses newly constructed by Willamette National employees.

Despite the problems attendant with the start-up of the mill, the facility was a model of utilization and efficiency. As Mel Cutler (who took over management of the Foster mill after Paul Morgan was transferred to Dallas) told a local newspaper reporter: "Let Chicago meat packers talk about using all but the squeal of the pig. We're even using the bark of the Douglas fir tree. That's utilization to the Nth degree. Waste is as obsolete around our plant as the Dodo bird."

It was to be George Gerlinger's last mill. For in October of 1948 Gerlinger died of a heart attack at the age of 72. He was eulogized by the Oregon press for his leadership on the Board of Forestry and in the industry. *The Oregonian* said of Gerlinger,

> By his own success in lumbering, Mr. Gerlinger proved that private enterprise can flourish without destruction of a resource that is a public legacy—Mr. Gerlinger's death removes one of the great figures in the fir industry, a man whose vision and sense of public responsibility equalled his genius as a builder and producer.

But he left an able, well-qualified successor. For indeed Bill Swindells had himself a job.

The Willamette National sawmill, just prior to its opening in 1947.

The construction of the Willamette National sawmill near Foster, September, 1946. From left to right: David Butler (with the Hill group), George Gerlinger, Maurie Clark, Bill Swindells, Charles Curley (with the Hills), Dave Mason (with the Hills), Phil Ray (with the Hills), Ralph King, Gene Ellis (with the Hills).

Stump strikes and all other manner of labor disruptions were common in the early years at Willamette National.

Art Morgans

Aaron Mercer

THE WILLAMETTE ECHO

Volume I   September, 1951   Number 1

*A 1951 edition of the Echo shows Willamette Valley's
related operations.*

CHAPTER 9

Setting the Stage for Growth

After Gerlinger died, Swindells took over as manager of the Willamette Valley Lumber Co. and Willamette National Lumber Co., including Corvallis Lumber and several logging operations.

Swindells began to look for opportunities for expansion. It was not long before he found one—the Santiam Lumber Company. Santiam Lumber was run by three very experienced timbermen—Carl Davis, Fred Powers and Coley Wheeler.

Fred Powers' father had founded the town of Powers on the southern Oregon coast around the turn of the century. In 1909 Carl Davis came to Powers from Minnesota and went to work for Smith-Powers as a timber cruiser.

In the early 20's Carl Davis and Fred Powers formed Powers-Davis, a contract logging company that worked all over southwestern Oregon. In 1935 the pair decided to try their luck at sawmilling and bought an old, out-of-date mill in Sweet Home, calling it the Santiam Lumber Company. They purchased some timberland; in fact, they logged what is now the southeast corner of Sweet Home. Finding it difficult to get reliable contract loggers, they moved the Powers-Davis Logging Company equipment to Sweet Home.

In 1940 the pair built the Powers-Davis Lumber Company in Lebanon, about 15 miles west of Sweet Home. A small operation, it had one of the first Swedish gang mills in the U.S.

In the meantime, Powers and Davis had been updating the Sweet Home mill. It had been completely modernized by 1946. That year, a fire burned the mill to the ground. The pair had insurance on the mill and operating insurance, so there was no financial loss.

Management did have one worry as it began to rebuild: Timber supply. Powers and Davis had tried to operate on fee timber. While they traded grades of logs with other companies, they had relied on their own lands for the bulk of their timber supply. Supply was getting low. That led to the merger in 1946 of the

Santiam Lumber Company of Sweet Home, the Powers-Davis Lumber Company of Lebanon and the Swamp Mountain Logging Company of Sweet Home. The new company was called Santiam Lumber Co.

Swamp Mountain was owned and operated by Coleman (Coley) H. Wheeler. Wheeler was from another old lumbering family which founded the town of Wheeler on Oregon's Nehalem Bay. Coley Wheeler had been involved in a variety of logging and lumbering operations. In 1940 he bought the Holmes Logging Company which operated out of Sweet Home. Wheeler shaped up the operations, doubling production in one month. That year he made the first contract arrangement with the Hills and began logging in the McDowell Creek area. He renamed his company McDowell Creek Logging. Two years later he changed the name of the company again to Swamp Mountain Logging and began logging Hill lands in the Swamp Mountain area, just 15 miles southeast of Sweet Home.

Santiam Lumber Company's profit-sharing contract with the Hills, similar to that held by Willamette National, made it an extremely attractive company to WVLCo.

In 1951 Fred Powers died. Carl Davis, himself up in years, was unwilling to take over operation of Santiam. The stock interest owned by Powers was absorbed by the remaining shareholders. The Willamette Valley Lumber Co. purchased the Davis interests, forming a new corporation with the same name, owned 40 percent by the Wheelers, 40 percent by WVLCo. and 20 percent by the Hills. Coley Wheeler was elected president of the new Santiam Lumber Co.; Bill Swindells, vice president; and Bill Schafer, a business associate of Wheeler, secretary-treasurer.

Richard Davis, son of Carl Davis, was the only member of the Powers or Davis families to remain with the new firm. L. R. Davidson and Harold Martin were key management personnel who came with the deal.

When WVLCo. bought into Santiam, the operation employed 850 people and produced 105 million board feet of lumber annually, about one-third of which was kiln-dried. The Sweet Home mill produced one million kilowatts of electricity each month—enough to run the mill and provide for some of the domestic needs of Sweet Home.

II

While the Willamette National mill at Foster and the Santiam Lumber Co. could rely at least temporarily on timber supply from their local area, WVLCo. and the Corvallis mill were beginning to find timber supply tight.

By the late 1940's WVLCo. was buying logs all over western Oregon. Jordan W. "Jay" Johnson, the Company's log buyer and reload manager, purchased logs out of the Coos Bay, Roseburg and Eugene areas, operating the Winchester and Cheshire reloads. These open market purchases helped extend fee-owned timber.

During that era, the Company began to develop 10-year logging plans for Dallas and 5-year logging plans for Corvallis. But even as early as 1945, the future of Corvallis was clouded. Its equipment was woefully out of date and inefficient. The mill had little fee timber left and competition for open market sales in the area was ferocious. It made little sense to modernize. Management considered Corvallis a "liquidating mill"—one that would log the last of its lands and what open market stumpage it could purchase, then shut down.

After the decision was made to close Corvallis, WVLCo. began an aggressive search for timberlands. With a conservative dividend policy, WVLCo. put a portion of its profits into timberland purchases beginning in 1947.

In 1949 the Company hired a forester, Gene Knudson, whose main job was to take a look at timber sales and land acquisitions. Knudson had been with the U.S. Bureau of Land Management (formerly the O&C Administration) and later with Dave Mason's consulting firm, Mason, Bruce and Girard.

Knudson tried to buy land for the value of the merchantable timber on it, essentially paying nothing for the land itself.

While there were many companies in the market for timberlands during this era, WVLCo.'s acquisition policies were considerably different from its competitors.

Large tracts of forest lands offered for sale were often a part of a lumber company's holdings. These holdings would usually contain a sawmill and timberlands, a portion of which were logged over. Many companies would purchase an outfit and run the sawmill until the timber was liquidated, then shut it down. However, WVLCo. would purchase this kind of operation and close down the sawmill almost immediately, preferring to process the timber in its own efficient facilities.

Another significant difference between WVLCo. purchases and those of other companies was the rate at which the lands were logged. Some companies borrowed against timber stumpage on the lands for funds to purchase the property. That meant they had to harvest the timber almost immediately to pay off the loan. WVLCo. took advantage of many of these deals by purchasing stumpage from companies in this position.

On its own purchased land, however, the Company was extremely conservative. It would log for a year or two to reduce debt, then begin worrying about future timber supply and back off, leaving a substantial portion of the timber for future logging.

This concern for the future was again reflected in a change made in planning for logging. By the time the Corvallis mill had closed in April of 1955, the 10-year logging plan for the Dallas mill had been dropped. Foresters decided the Company was going to be around for more than 10 years, so they needed to work toward a sustained yield harvest plan to keep the Company in timber forever.

Another demonstration of that dedication to the future was the Company's first major purchase of cut-over lands. This land, 8,180 acres owned by a Grand Rapids, Michigan furniture company, had been logged, but contained thrifty young stands of Douglas fir and substantial residual timber. The land was purchased mainly for future timber supply, made feasible years earlier by George Gerlinger's insistence on a tax to help landowners maintain cut-over lands.

The next few years brought many opportunities for expansion of the Company's timber base and WVLCo. management kept itself in a financial position to take advantage of these opportunities as they arose.

The Watzek's 7,000 acre Roaring River Tree Farm near Snow Peak was purchased in 1955. The next year WVLCo. purchased the Fischer Lumber Company, then resold the mill to Fischer, keeping the company's 22,000 acres of timberland. A year later the Company bought the L.H.L. Lumber Co. (Linke, Haynes and Lantis) in Carlton, some 34 miles north of Dallas. The operation was purchased mainly for its 24,000 acres of timberland. But WVLCo. management made an agreement with the owners to run a portion of the mill for five years. Mill manager Ed Cutler (son of

Mel who had worked in the Dallas and Corvallis mills) closed the large log mill soon after WVLCo. purchased the facility, continued running a small log mill and constructed a veneer plant. At the end of the five years, the mill and veneer plant were closed. The timberlands became the Trask Tree Farm.

In 1959 the remainder of the Hammond lands, the half the Company didn't purchase in 1938, were acquired from Georgia-Pacific.

III

In the meantime, the Hill contract was modified to extend its duration. Originally the contract was to last 15 years. At the end of that period, the contract read, the entire Hill ownership was to have been logged. As time wore on, it became obvious that this provision in the contract was to the advantage of neither party. It would make more sense to allow Willamette National to purchase on the open market occasionally. The Hills could still share in the profits of the mill, yet maintain their timber income over a longer period. Willamette National's contract was renegotiated in 1957 to provide a maximum and minimum cut each year. Santiam Lumber similarly modified its contract. The contracts were to last until every acre of timberland was harvested once. (Consolidated into one contract in 1967 at the time of the merger, the Hill arrangement was still in effect on the Company's diamond anniversary in 1980.)

IV

The purchase of an interest in the Santiam Lumber Co., the acquisition of timberlands, the extension of the Hill contract and the pruning of withering branches like Carlton and Corvallis placed WVLCo. in an excellent position for growth.

Gene D. Knudson

Coley Wheeler, Sr.

William Swindells, Sr.

CHAPTER 10

The Western Kraft Corporation and the Western Corrugated Box Companies

Willamette Valley Lumber Co. had been interested in papermaking since the mid-1920's. The Polk County amalgamation, discussed prior to the Depression, had included a proposal for pooling funds for a paper mill. When the amalgamation fell through, management continued to seek a similar opportunity. But a paper mill, even then, was a phenomenal investment and small lumber companies like WVLCo. didn't have the capital resources or the raw material for such a venture.

In 1950 seven Oregon lumber firms, including WVLCo., Willamette National and Santiam, formed the Wood Utilization Promotion Committee to determine the feasibility of pooling their resources to construct a pulp mill, probably in the Albany area. The seven companies had discussions with Crown Zellerbach and several Midwest paper companies about possible partnerships. After several years the plan was dropped.

But WVLCo.'s interest in papermaking continued. The Company and its related mills were producing huge quantities of chips. It only made sense to put those chips to work in a family-related paper mill.

Swindells talked to several paper industry consultants and each said it wasn't feasible to build a small paper mill. A minimal starter mill, they said, should be able to produce 250 tons a day with an initial investment of about $25 million. Swindells felt the consultants were quoting such high construction costs because they wanted to keep WVLCo. out of the paper business.

One day in 1953 Swindells got a phone call from Dave Mason, who had served as a raw materials consultant to the Wood Utilization Promotion Committee and represented the Hill interests. "Why don't you come on over, Bill, there's someone in my office I think you should talk to."

He was referring to Ira Keller. At 54 years of age, Ira Keller had left a lucrative position as executive vice president of Container Corporation to look for an opportunity in the Pacific

Northwest. He wanted to stay in the paper business with an operation he could help build.

After a brief discussion, Keller said he'd make a preliminary study of the feasibility of a moderate-sized mill. His subsequent report indicated that a 125 ton per day kraft linerboard mill could be built for less than $10 million.

WVLCo. and Santiam Lumber hired Keller as a consultant to draw up detailed plans for the mill.

The Western Kraft Corporation was formed on October 21, 1954. Wilson W. Clark was chairman of the board; Ira Keller, president; Robert V. Hansberger, executive vice president (Hansberger had been associated with Keller at Container Corporation); William Swindells and Coley Wheeler, vice presidents; and Maurice Clark and Robert C. Kirkwood (brother-in-law to Bill Swindells, and an attorney who was at the time serving as controller for the state of California), directors.

Willamette Valley Lumber Co. owned 67 percent of Western Kraft stock; Coley Wheeler, 15 percent; Ira Keller, 15 percent; Bill Swindells, 3 percent.

When engineering estimates under the direction of John Beaver were complete, it appeared that close to $8 million would be needed to build the mill and provide working capital. About $3.8 million was furnished by stockholders. A $4.5 million loan by Northwest Mutual Life Insurance of Milwaukee provided the remainder of the capital.

Selection of a site was probably the easiest part of the whole process. The mill had to be in line with the flow of chips from related operations. It had to be on a rail line and a river. Jefferson, Lebanon, Sweet Home and Corvallis had been given consideration, but a 200-acre site three miles north of Albany was selected. The site was located between the Willamette River and the Southern Pacific North-South mainline and was only 38 miles from the farthest "family" related sawmill. Purchase was negotiated by Ira Keller's son, Dick.

Ground was broken in February of 1955, and the mill started making linerboard in September of that year. It was running in the black by year's end. In 1956 capacity was expanded to 180 tons per day.

It was the first paper mill in the United States to make paper exclusively from chips made from the residue of sawmills and plywood plants and never vary from that fiber source. Unlike other mills, Western Kraft was built with no log deck, log pond or wood room. Some critics doubted the mill could succeed on that basis. But its expansion and continued operation proved it a model of efficient use of the forest's fiber.

II

The Western Kraft Albany mill was a merchant mill—it produced kraft linerboard for conversion by others. Even before ground was broken, Keller had received informal commitments through his Western Sales Co. for about 85 percent of the mill's capacity. A study done by a New York consulting firm had shown that the deficit of linerboard for conversion on the West Coast was nearly twice the anticipated output of the facility.

However, soon after the mill began operating, several of Albany's major customers were purchased, one by one, by larger paper companies which did not renew contracts with Western Kraft. In addition, a major West Coast linerboard manufacturer arbitrarily cut its prices by 10 percent and other mills followed suit. Orders and profit were cut substantially.

Future direction soon became obvious: It was no longer profitable to operate a merchant mill on the West Coast. Western Kraft had to enter the box business and build or purchase corrugated container plants to use linerboard produced by the mill.

III

Early in 1955 the Western Corrugated Box Co. was formed. Ira Keller was chairman; Roy Fefley, president; Rudy Gingg, vice president; George Karr, secretary-treasurer.

The new company bought 16 acres in San Leandro, California (in the Bay area) for its first corrugated container plant. It immediately began construction and started box production 120 days later. The plant had been planned simultaneously with the Albany mill, but began producing boxes before the mill began making paper.

In fact, San Leandro's salesmen began selling boxes before there was even a plant in which to make them. Prior to the plant's opening, corrugated containers were manufactured by other companies with Western Corrugated's box certification stamp. By the time the plant began its own production, the salesmen had sold enough boxes to cover all their salaries and expenses.

From the very beginning the plant attracted some strong, stable customers like Lipton Tea, Folger's coffee, Stokely Van Camp and Del Monte.

In 1956 Dick Keller opened a box plant in Beaverton, Oregon, just west of Portland, using contacts made through customers of the San Leandro plant to develop business. This was again a separate company called Western Corrugated of Oregon. It operated out of a small building with used equipment designed to make standard shipping containers for food canneries.

The year Beaverton opened, the San Leandro plant became the second corrugated box plant in the world to purchase a new machine known as a flexo. The flexo took processes previously done by two machines and merged them into one. The flexo could print, score, slot, glue and fold all in one process. It was a tremendous advance in container making. The third flexo ever made went into the Beaverton plant, giving both plants a tremendous advantage in efficiency over other West Coast operations.

In 1958 a tiny sheet plant was opened in Wenatchee, Washington to serve the needs of the produce industry in eastern Washington.

Another cell was split off the San Leandro plant in 1959 with the opening of the Compton, California plant. This was a division of Western Kraft. Working from San Leandro's southern California customers as a base, the plant developed a solid list of industrial, glass and produce customers.

Also in 1959, Western Corrugated of Oregon was liquidated and the Beaverton plant became wholly owned by Western Kraft.

IV

At the beginning, the Albany mill had problems with the quality of the Tuff-Tare linerboard it produced. The product occasionally had difficulty meeting Mullen (strength) tests. When C.R. "Neil" Duffie, a chemical engineer, took over as mill manager from Hansberger in 1957, he took steps to improve the quality of the mill's product. This included construction of a $100,000 lab which contained all the latest box testing and development equipment to insure the quality of the paper and the strength of the completed corrugated container. Felix Hammack was named technical director in charge of the lab, which opened in 1959.

In addition to Hammack, a solid, technically based crew was being cultivated at the mill. Hod Reins, Tom Syme, Earl Shook, Skeets Morrison and others brought their technical and papermaking backgrounds to Albany to help stabilize the operation.

V

In 1960 one of Western Kraft's linerboard customers in California, Sam Kalof of Kalof Pulp and Paper Company, was having financial difficulties.

Kalof owned recycled corrugating medium and linerboard mills in Port Hueneme (north of Los Angeles near Oxnard) and in Richmond. He also owned four corrugated container plants: Hand Container and Quaker Container, across the alley from each other in Vernon; a plant adjacent to the Richmond mill; and Cadillac Container, alongside the Port Hueneme mill. He was a steady customer for Western Kraft linerboard, so he came to the Company with an offer to sell.

Western Kraft didn't have the cash to buy Kalof's operation, so management negotiated a 10-year lease of the Kalof properties with purchase at the end of the lease. The Port Hueneme recycling mill was closed prior to the lease agreement. (It remained closed for several years thereafter.) The medium mill in Richmond continued to make corrugating medium for the California plants. Walt Heinemann moved there from Albany as manager with Orville Latimer as superintendent and the pair thoroughly upgraded the facility. Cadillac Container was closed and its business divided between San Leandro, Compton, Richmond, Hand and Quaker.

In 1961 Western Corrugated opened a sheet plant in Sacramento, once again putting its experience with agricultural customers to good use. Kalof's Richmond corrugated container plant was closed and equipment from the facility used to start the Sacramento plant. The Sacramento plant concentrated on fruit and vegetable canners and dried fruit producers in the Sacramento and San Joaquin Valleys.

VI

Western Kraft's growth had been substantial. In five short years the Company had grown from a single merchant mill to a mill producing for seven affiliated corrugated container plants.

Some basic philosophies about future growth had been learned from the experience. Paper mills with no frills were to be a trademark of Western Kraft. The Albany mill was the only Company paper mill to be born with a merchant mill concept. Subsequent mills and subsequent expansions at Albany were to spring from a healthy internal demand: Company-owned converting plants creating a need for paper production.

VII

The growth of Western Kraft was due mainly to Ira Keller's jack-of-all-trades ability. He was at home in a paper mill, box plant, customer's manufacturing facility or its corporate headquarters. He dug into the West Coast market and came up with steady customers. His marketing strategy was simple and direct. "We must deliver a good product at a fair price on time. Our sales representatives must reflect our principles and character. They must know our business thoroughly and be capable of rendering a real service to our customers. They must be proud to bear our name and strong enough to fight for good orders for us and good service and value for their customers."

Keller used his own personal influence to lure many good people in the industry to Western Kraft. His motto for personnel management was "fair play, fair pay, recognition as individuals, opportunities for advancement and reasonable job security."

"Western Kraft," Keller told his employees, "was founded as a Declaration of Independence against the rigidities of the large corporation. I think, therefore, we have a special obligation to preserve the freedom of initiative of the small enterprise and still achieve a sufficient growth to insure our competitive strength." And, indeed, Western Kraft had that competitive strength in just a few short years.

Ira Keller

The Albany mill, 1955, the first paper mill in the
United States to make paper exclusively from chips
made from the residue of sawmills and plywood plants
and never vary from that source.

When Neil Duffie took over management of the Albany
mill, quality of the product was greatly improved.

In 1959, the mill installed an extensive development
lab. Shown left to right, Robert Campbell, Ed
Kirkpatrick and Felix Hammack.

CHAPTER 11

Expansion on a Growing Base: The decade of the 1950's.

Probably no period in the Company's history was more influential in the development of future direction than the decade of the 1950's. This period was one of increasing the fee timber base while developing new product lines made from waste products from lumber and plywood operations. The era saw some significant steps in the development of vertical integration.

II

Plywood was not new in the 50's. The first plywood in Oregon was made in Portland for display at the 1905 Lewis and Clark Exposition.

Up until World War II, plywood was used mainly for decorative purposes. Any small imperfections were filled and the sheets were sanded.

But during World War II plywood sheathing was developed. Sheathing became a competitor with lumber as it could be used to "sheathe" the outside of a building—as wall sheathing, subflooring or roof decking. It was much simpler to use than lumber because of its convenient 4′ by 8′ size.

Sheathing interested WVLCo. and Santiam Lumber, so the companies began to look at Western Veneer in Griggs, Oregon, located between Lebanon and Albany near the Snow Peak pond. In the early 50's there were probably 90 plywood plants in the U.S. but only a few were making sheathing.

The plant at Griggs, owned by Harold Jones, had opened in January 1949. It pioneered in using cull and salvage logs which were not suitable for conventional sawmills or plywood plants. Other plywood plants used peeler logs—the very highest grade of log. However, Western Veneer could use defective logs and produce a 50-50 mix of sanded plywood and sheathing.

Other mills wouldn't bother with inferior logs because they would spin out or break up on the lathe, creating handling problems. The Griggs plant was geared for using cull and salvage logs and made up for the expense of extra handling by the low prices paid for the logs.

Because of the nature of the log, there was a great deal of waste. So chip and hog fuel production were important parts of the Griggs operation.

There couldn't have been a plywood plant to better fit WVLCo.'s and Santiam's operations, because it could give them an outlet for their cull logs, vastly improving utilization. So in December, 1953 the companies bought Western Veneer, renaming it Western Veneer and Plywood.

III

Soon after the purchase, Western Veneer and Plywood found itself in a bitter debate that ended in court.

The Douglas Fir Plywood Association (DFPA) was the only plywood inspection agency in the Douglas fir region of the Northwest. Douglas fir plywood destined for construction meeting Building Code requirements had to be certified by DFPA as meeting U.S. Bureau of Standards' requirements. The grade of the plywood had to be stamped on the surface of each panel along with DFPA's certification.

For the most part, DFPA members were Washington plywood plants. Washington had more plywood plants than Oregon because the timber was finer—not as old as in Oregon and with less rot. High grade peelers were abundant.

The Griggs plant began to use white speck veneer in the inner plies of both sanded plywood and sheathing. Old growth trees sometimes contain a fungus that destroys little spots of wood fiber, leaving a white speck. A log from an infected tree will produce veneer with tiny white polka-dots throughout.

DFPA questioned the use of white speck veneer. Its members were concerned that the use of white speck would destroy growing builder confidence in the quality and strength of plywood.

So DFPA threatened to take away the mill's inspection stamps, a step that could have taken Western Veneer and Plywood right out of the plywood market. Mill manager Harry Graham sent samples of white speck plywood to DFPA headquarters in Washington for testing. The tests showed the plywood with white speck inner plies was in most cases stronger than required. The tests did not satisfy DFPA members.

DFPA then sent samples of veneer containing white speck back to the U.S. Forest Service's forest products lab in Madison, Wisconsin for testing. The first lab experiments were a failure because the lab used only the amount of adhesive required by standard to make their test plywood. The mill had discovered that white specks absorbed glue, so more was necessary. The resulting panels were actually stronger because of the extra adhesive penetration. Graham himself went back to Madison and showed them the mill's technique for making plywood. The result, the forest products lab certified, was plywood that was up to specification.

But DFPA refused to go along with the results and revoked the mill's grade stamps and certification. For a while the mill made a stamp of its own. But the plywood could not be used in construction meeting Building Code requirements. In the meantime, Western Veneer and Plywood went to court to require DFPA to return the certification stamps.

Western Veneer and Plywood asked an eastern agency, Timber Engineering Co. (TECO), to again study white speck plywood and comment upon its properties. Another plywood plant owned by a former WVLCo. employee, Jack Brandis, had begun to use white speck and joined in paying for the $46,000 study.

The result of the study was something DFPA hadn't counted on—direct competition. TECO was well-respected as a testing lab in the East. After its study showed white speck plywood met standards, TECO offered its services as a testing and grade certification agency to the Griggs plant, replacing DFPA, in 1957. Western Veneer and Plywood was TECO's first western grade maintenance client, and a TECO technician was stationed at Griggs on a full-time basis to assure the quality of the product.

The result of the white speck controversy was an important one for the concept of log utilization, extending the timber resource by using cull logs that would otherwise have been left in the woods to rot. All grading agencies soon allowed white speck in inner plies and it became commonly used by all plywood manufacturers.

IV

The Griggs plant had met management's expectations, teaching WVLCo. and Santiam production skills and sales techniques. Growing confidence in this market led to the construction of a sheathing plant on the Dallas sawmill grounds which opened on August 15, 1955. Willamette National followed with its sheathing plant at Foster in September of 1958, and Santiam Lumber opened the Sweet Home plywood plant in May, 1959. Lebanon Plywood was constructed by Santiam in an old potato field near the Lebanon sawmill, opening in May of 1961. Generally speaking, when plywood plants were opened, the sawmills' production output was reduced so that overall log demand was maintained.

In 1963 the Santiam Lumber Co. constructed Mohawk Veneer in Springfield, just east of Eugene, to make green veneer for Springfield area plywood plants. In 1966 the operation expanded into a full plywood plant.

V

This growing network of related sawmills and plywood plants produced an important by-product from mill waste: Chips, which were put to use when the Western Kraft paper mill opened. The paper mill provided WVLCo. and Santiam with an opportunity to expand their profits without requiring an expansion of the timberland base.

After Western Kraft opened, management began to study another wood product made with waste from plywood plants and sawmills—particleboard. It could be made without the need to expand the timberland base from scraps of mill leftovers not suitable for chips for paper-making.

In the mid-1950's furniture and cabinet makers were beginning to look seriously at the uses of particleboard. The use of solid wood in these items was becoming prohibitively expensive, and manufacturers were interested in particleboard as a substitute.

Bill Swindells studied the market and particleboard manufacturing for quite some time, and finally WVLCo. and Santiam Lumber decided to take a chance. In August of 1959 they formed the Wood Fiberboard Company. Bill Swindells was president; Coley Wheeler, vice president; A.R. Morgans, secretary.

A German, Ernst Greten, had just developed a new air flotation system for making particleboard which seemed quite superior to the processes used in the United States. This system could automatically put the fines (the smallest particles) on the outside and the increasingly larger particles to the center in one step, creating a strong, well-integrated board with a smooth surface.

This German "Bison" process had not been used in the United States. Bill Swindells, Jr. sent several loads of Douglas fir shavings to Germany to see if the process would work on fir. Tests produced an extremely fine board and the German company was as excited about the prospects as WVLCo. and Santiam were about the product. The German machinery was very versatile, making a variety of thicknesses and widths. The board was smooth, showed excellent structural qualities, an unusually high internal bond, and good machining and screw holding ability.

Wood Fiberboard contracted with the German company to produce a turnkey operation—the Germans agreed to set up the machines and fine-tune them, then turn the plant over. The cost: $1,750,000.

A 15-acre plant site was purchased less than a quarter of a mile south of the Western Kraft paper mill near Albany and construction of the building began. So did the headaches.

The German motors on the machines were too light to do the job. Once the motors were right, the machines just wouldn't operate properly. They could not produce the quality of board they had produced in their tests in Germany. The opening date of the plant was pushed further and further back. Finally, depending upon who tells the story, the Germans were thrown out or they threw up their hands in disgust and left. Swindells went back to New York to find out, among other things, if Wood Fiberboard could sue the makers of the German Bison system.

After the Germans left, the plant's tinkerers took over and began to tune up the plant to produce an acceptable grade of particleboard. The plant had been scheduled to open in April, 1960. It produced its first board in August. The first TECO tested board was sold in December. Yet it was a far cry from the quality of particleboard made today.

In fact, Bill Affolter, salesman for Duraflake (as the particleboard was named) was questioned about the properties of the new board at a Company Christmas party. Wood Fiberboard had made little puzzles for the party by cutting a small board with a jigsaw. Partygoers found their dinner partners by matching jigsaw pieces. Affolter was seated next to a dyed-in-the-wool plywood plant man who took a look at the new particleboard and said, "Well, what's going to happen when this stuff gets wet?" Affolter assured him the particleboard could take a bit of moisture and dunked a piece in his coffee cup to prove his point. The particleboard disintegrated in the coffee.

The product rapidly improved and soon began to gain acceptance with manufacturers, becoming the standard for the industry. Three types of particleboard were produced at first: Duraflake, Duraflake Underlayment and Duraflake Furniture. Duraflake Furniture was very popular with furniture manufacturers because it was extremely smooth and could accept laminates well.

TECO set up a permanent lab inside the plant for continuous testing. Y.C. Cheo was hired as technical director at the plant. He developed his own lab and was responsible for many of the improvements made in the board over the years.

Wood Fiberboard began to be recognized as a leader in engineering and technology in the particleboard industry. For many years it was the nation's largest producer of particleboard products under one roof. The tinkerers at the plant who brought the German Bison system to life made many improvements in the particleboard-making process. They improved the forming station, the press, the design of the saw and made many other modifications to the system. Wood Fiberboard was the first particleboard plant to have a sander dust burning boiler and the first to have steam coils to heat the dryer.

The slogan used by the sales team under George Swindells (Bill Swindells' second son) was "Wood isn't what it used to be—it's better." The sales staff found Duraflake's product was so superior to other particleboards that they didn't have to compete. Their role was to challenge markets dominated by lumber and plywood. They traveled around the United States looking for applications of lumber or plywood that could be converted to particleboard. One early victory was particleboard ping pong tables. Once the sales team convinced one manufacturer that he could save $1,000 a carload by using particleboard for his tables, the rest of the market was easy to crack.

By June of 1961 a third shift was added, making Duraflake an around-the-clock operation, giving WVLCo., Santiam Lumber and other local mills a further outlet for former waste products.

In 1961 the plant produced 18.5 million square feet. A second production line was added in 1963, bringing 1964's total production to 57.5 million feet.

A third line was added in 1970 when Tom Buglione was made manager. Floyd Vike and a growing sales staff sold 122 million feet that year. No expansion was ever undertaken until the sales department was confident it could find markets for the increased capacity.

VI

With chips being converted to paper and shavings to particleboard, WVLCo. and Santiam were becoming highly efficient operations. But one day Ted Huntley, manager of the Foster plywood plant, watched a fellow load up the plant's peeler cores (the core of the log left after veneer is peeled off). The fellow came daily to pick up the cores, haul them to a mill where he'd cut them into 2" x 4" studs, then ship them to Lebanon for planing. Huntley got to thinking that if the fellow could make a profit doing all that hauling, then surely a little scrag mill on the premises at Foster could be profitable.

Huntley sold the project to management and it was a resounding success, used as a pattern in later years for similar installations in many Company plants. Like chips and shavings, peeler cores provided an opportunity for producing profit without increasing the resource base.

VII

By the early 1960's WVLCo., Santiam and their related companies had undergone extensive changes—developing a growing base of timberlands and a network of efficient wood processing facilities.

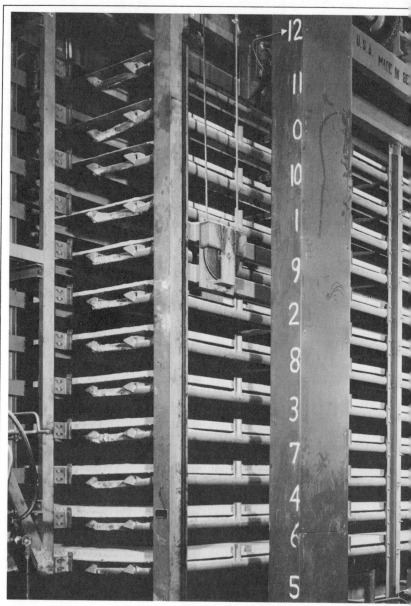

All of the equipment at the Duraflake plant was fabricated in Germany and took American tinkerers many months to render operational.

109

CHAPTER 12

Western Kraft

When the Albany paper mill was constructed, the concept of air and water pollution control was new. Companies were beginning to experiment with air pollution control, but systems were crude and unreliable. Consequently, when the mill opened no one with any sense of smell could deny that the mill stunk. Locals would wrinkle their noses and say, "That's the smell of money."

Soon after the mill was constructed, Oregon's north-south freeway, I-5, was completed, bringing increased traffic right into the mill's backyard. The smell and the mill's steam plumes gradually attracted state-wide attention.

At first, a portion of the smell was due to the operators' lack of familiarity with the equipment. As employees became more familiar with the controls, some of the problem was eliminated. But the nose could hardly tell the difference.

Like many other paper mills around the country, the Albany mill became a symbol of industrial pollution for environmental groups. Governor Tom McCall called Western Kraft "a stinking cancer on the broad green bosom of the Willamette Valley."

Felix Hammack, who had been promoted to mill manager, spent most of his time on public relations. Educators, students, state agencies and newsmen were invited to the plant to discuss air quality concerns. When mill employees noticed a photographer on the freeway aiming his camera at the plume, Hammack would soon be told, and he'd drive out to the freeway to invite the photographer in for a personal tour. Invariably, this either dampened the photographer's enthusiasm or changed his opinion.

During the first 11 years of operation the mill spent hundreds of thousands of dollars on improvements aimed at pollution control. In 1972 the mill completed a $16 million expansion including $5.8 million for air pollution control and over $350,000 for water pollution control. The Oregon Department of Environmental Quality certified that the mill met emission requirements slated to go into effect in 1975. The new controls reduced the emission level over 95 percent. Slowly, Oregon's environmental groups dropped their banners and went on to tackle other causes.

II

The mill's expansion programs were fueled by market developments in the converting plants. Corrugated containers were not the only items using kraft paper. Over the years, Ira Keller and Dick Keller (who later became a senior vice president of the Company) had considered a number of kraft-using industries as possibilities. They studied the making of kraft tape, multi-wall bags and a variety of other products. The most promising use of kraft was the manufacture of sacks and grocery bags. The brown bag industry was the second largest user of kraft paper and it was growing rapidly in the early 1960's. It was a simple business and appeared to be a practical enterprise for a paper and box maker with no experience, no skills and no customers in the retail business.

Western Kraft constructed a very small bag plant in the corrugated container plant in Beaverton in 1961. It was a simple operation employing only 15 people at first.

Initially, the plant was much like others across the United States—it made a variety of grocery and department store bags and sold them through jobbers. Most bag plants during the era were strictly production oriented with no sales staff.

As the Company grew more familiar with the bag business, it became obvious that there was a better marketing technique. The plant hired a modest sales force and instructed the salesmen to go for truckload and larger orders, working directly with the customer. The technique proved profitable for the Company and its customers.

The bag division's biggest concern was the need to maintain quality. As a quality improvement program, the division began to print the bag machine tender's name on the bottom of each bag. The employee's pride in his product kept quality high. While many companies do this today, Western Kraft was the first.

Yet another innovative sales strategy was the development of the 75 lb. grocery bag. For heavy loads many bag companies were constructing the 40-40 duplex (two 40 lb. pieces of sack kraft were spot glued together, then formed into a sack). Others were recommending double-bagging, using two 57 lb.

sacks. The Albany mill had installed its #2 paper machine in 1963 and it had the capability of making 75 lb. sack kraft. Chuck Carlbom, manager of the bag division, sold the idea of a single 75 lb. sack to the military for use in its commissaries, then to civilian grocers. This kind of innovative marketing led to rapid growth at the Beaverton plant and at the Los Angeles area plant which opened in 1966.

III

In the meantime, the West Coast corrugated container plants were growing with vigor.

In 1963 a corrugator was added to the Sacramento plant. Warehouse and sales operations in Washington state were carving out a market for eventual construction of a container plant there.

About this time management began eyeing the Port Hueneme paper mill which had been closed when Western Kraft acquired Kalof's properties. With West Coast operations expanding, there was a greater need for corrugating medium. The mill had been designed to make corrugating medium, linerboard and folding carton material from recycled boxes and newspapers, abundant in the Los Angeles area. Leo Dozoretz, who had come to the Company with the Kalof properties, was sent to Port Hueneme to investigate re-opening the mill.

The mill had been closed for nearly five years, sitting in the salty sea air. But Dozoretz was optimistic that the mill could be put back in shape. He got rid of all equipment not directly related to the manufacture of medium. Repair crews parlayed the remaining equipment into the fastest cylinder-type paper machine in the world.

In the early 1960's it became evident that the Western Kraft Corrugated Container Division was a resounding success. With plants in Oregon, northern and southern California, and sales areas staked out in Washington, Western Kraft had covered the West Coast market. It had increased its share of the market from 5.5 percent in 1959 to 10 percent in 1962. Management felt further major expansions would have to be undertaken in other market areas.

Ira Keller had worked in the Chicago area for years and knew the market intimately. He felt that if Western Kraft were to expand beyond the West Coast, it could do it by locating in the industry-rich Chicago area. The Elk Grove plant, just north of Chicago, opened in 1963 as a sheet plant, but a corrugator was added shortly thereafter.

That same year Western Kraft purchased Pak-Rite, a corrugated container plant in Melrose Park, Illinois and in 1964 it purchased a minority interest in Druth Packaging, with a container plant in Chicago and a packaging plant in Brooklyn, New York. A third sheet plant was opened in Rockford, Illinois in 1966. All of these affiliations were undertaken to sell sheets from the Elk Grove corrugator (Western Kraft's interest in all three was later sold).

At this point Keller found himself in a difficult position. With no Company-related paper mill in the East, further growth would be dependent upon the whims of the paper market. Yet the Company did not have adequate converting capacity in the East to warrant construction of a mill. So Ira Keller looked up an old friend.

Sam Davis had worked with Keller at Container Corp. but left in the mid-1940's to purchase the Corrugated Container Company (later called Corco). By 1964 Davis' company had three Midwest container plants. Davis had given some thought to construction of a paper mill, but he didn't have the converting capacity to warrant construction of a mill or the technical capabilities. In November 1965 Western Kraft and the Corrugated Container Company formed WesCor.

WesCor was a 50-50 joint venture between Western Kraft and Corco to construct a corrugating medium mill in the Midwest. Sam Davis was president; C.R. Duffie, executive vice president; George Wilders (president and general manager of Corco), secretary-treasurer; and Bob Feltner (vice president of Corco), vice president and general manager.

The mill was to be a neutral-sulphite semi-chemical pulp and paper mill. Davis favored a site in Indiana for the mill. But Neil Duffie had heard about some industrial sites along the Ohio River in Hancock County, Kentucky. After checking the Indiana site Duffie drove to Hancock County to see what was available. He found a parcel of land near Hawesville, located between the Ohio River and L & N Railroad, off a state highway route and near a toll bridge being constructed across the Ohio. The site was perfect.

Engineers flooded into Hawesville and talks were rapidly underway with local utilities and the L & N. Sam Davis went to see the owner of the property to negotiate the sale. The owner agreed with Davis on a price and asked for a check. When Davis said he'd have to mail him the check, the farmer said the deal was off. On the chance that the farmer might not be kidding, Davis wrote him a personal check on the spot to purchase the property.

Like most Company projects, WesCor was built with economy in mind. Most paper mills went first class; Western Kraft went tourist, but always arrived at the same destination at the same time. Most paper machines in the industry are named and a bronze nameplate is affixed to the machine. WesCor folks wanted to name their machine "The Kentucky Colonel", but there was no money in the budget for a bronze nameplate. One day during construction one of the workers said he knew a fellow who could make a nameplate out of wood that could be painted to look just like bronze. Engineers Ted Kasparek, Hod Reins and Norm Schmidt were skeptical, but the price was definitely right. The nameplate was carved, painted and mounted. It fooled Neil Duffie, who asked the engineers how they'd been able to buy a bronze plaque on their limited budget. (The wooden plaque was scorched in a fire and replaced with another, which still fools papermakers touring WesCor.)

Kentucky's first pulp and paper mill cost $9.3 million to construct. The mill opened in April of 1967, producing 200 tons per day of corrugating medium. Half of the output was sold to Western Kraft; the other half to Corco.

The Hawesville area was primarily agricultural, growing sorghum, corn and tobacco. Industry consisted of furniture manufacturers and sawmills. The bulk of the mill's employees came from the local area, but technicians and engineers were lured to the area by advertisements promising life in "a pleasant community north of the southern summers and south of the northern winters." Employees of the Albany mill traveled to Kentucky to help teach the necessary papermaking and maintenance skills. Skeets Morrison was named superintendent.

WesCor used 75 percent virgin hardwood fiber and 25 percent recycled fiber. But there was a tremendous potential for procurement of hardwood chips. Local sawmills had no outlet for their left-over fiber. Farmers had thousands of acres of unused woodlots suitable for pulpwood.

Western Kraft management knew there were a number of small paper companies in the Midwest that purchased significant quantities of pulp. Studies had shown that there was enough fiber in the Hawesville area to support more than one pulp and paper mill. It became obvious to management that there was a demand for pulp and that one day soon a pulp or paper company was going to build facilities near WesCor. Western Kraft wanted to be the one to do it. Talk of building a bleached pulp mill started before WesCor was finished.

Building a bleached pulp mill went against the rule management had made after the construction of Albany: Never build a mill without paper converting capacity. However, this mill filled such an obvious need that the rule was broken. Western Kraft officially announced plans to build a bleached pulp mill right next to the corrugating medium mill in Skillman's Bottom. Several of the Company's engineers and their families moved to the Hawesville area to supervise construction and get the mill off to a good start.

The Market Pulp Division began production in June of 1969. It had a 230 ton per day capacity with an employment of 140. The mill's entire production was marketed by Gottesman and Company of New York.

By sharing chip handling facilities with WesCor and practicing other typical Western Kraft economies, the Market Pulp Division had a first class mill with a tourist class tab.

Capital investment per ton at this mill was extremely low. Unfortunately, start-up was very difficult and the market for bleached pulp took a dive soon after the mill began to produce good pulp. After these temporary set-backs the mill proved a solid investment.

IV

Once again the old bugaboo of timberlands reared its ugly head. There was an adequate supply of roundwood available from local farmers and chips from local wood manufacturing firms to fill the two mills' fiber appetites. But what if a recession or a strike closed down local manufacturing operations? What if competition for wood fiber increased the price of residue fiber greatly?

During one bad winter, when snow and ice froze up the supply of chips to the mills, they resorted to chipping up used whisky barrels from Louisville for raw material. That experience further encouraged management to consider the purchase of timberlands.

As early as 1967 Knudson and Swindells urged WesCor to begin the purchase of timberlands as a backup for the Kentucky mills. As Corco was not convinced of the need for backup timberlands, Western Kraft began to purchase land in Kentucky on its own.

A few parcels were bought in Kentucky, but they were unsatisfactory both in price and quality of land. These were later sold. High quality land in central Tennessee could be purchased for around $25 an acre, so Western Kraft soon turned to this area. The first purchase in June of 1968 was the 13,189 acre Goodman Tract. As similar tracts became available in the area, they were purchased. Mayford Williams was hired as forester in charge. (On its 75th anniversary, Willamette owned 84,000 acres in Tennessee.)

By 1970 the Kentucky ventures were proving a resounding success. That sub-compact paper company spawned on the banks of an unpronounceable river in Oregon had become a major force in the pulp, paper and packaging industry.

The Port Hueneme recycling mill proved a boon to local recycling groups. One Boy Scout troop made enough money collecting newspapers for recycling to pay for a trip to Europe.

The Kentucky Colonel, posing with Ira Keller, Governor Breathitt and Katherine Peden of the Kentucky Department of Commerce.

CHAPTER 13

Growth by Joint Venture and Merger

The rapid growth of Santiam and WVLCo. during the 1950's and early 60's had been fueled by the expansion of the fee timber base and by the development of new products that didn't require additional fiber sources. Management was reluctant to continue that rate of growth without buying more timberlands. As forest land was becoming harder to find and as the Companies were developing tremendous capital needs for existing plant expansion and modernization, management had to develop some creative solutions in order to expand.

The solution management chose was the joint venture concept. WVLCo. and Santiam had a skilled pool of employees who knew every phase of the plywood and particleboard business. On the other hand, there were many lumber companies, even as late as the 60's, that had never ventured into plywood making, much less particleboard. Some of these companies had significant landholdings but were reluctant to diversify because they lacked technical knowledge. Management decided the road to expansion would lie in joining with these landholding lumber companies in joint venture plywood and particleboard operations.

Bill Swindells was looking at just such an opportunity in northern California when fate, again in the form of Mason, Bruce and Girard, offered another option. Karl Henze of the consulting firm suggested that a lumber company in Bend, Oregon, Brooks-Scanlon, might be just the partner Swindells was looking for. Brooks-Scanlon was interested in making plywood with its fir logs and particleboard with waste from its pine sawmill. After a series of discussions, a joint venture called Brooks-Willamette Corporation was formed in November, 1964 with Bill Swindells as president, Conley Brooks and John Hollern as vice presidents, and A.R. Morgans as secretary-treasurer.

Sam Robb, industrial relations man for WVLCo., was sent to Bend to manage Brooks-Willamette under the leadership of Bill Swindells, Jr.

Brooks-Willamette immediately announced plans to build particleboard and plywood plants in the Bend area. However, plans were changed early the next year when Brooks-Willamette purchased the Tite Knot sawmill and the Dahl Pine veneer plant in Redmond, just 16 miles northeast of Bend.

The Dahl Pine veneer plant was still under construction at the time of its sale to Brooks-Willamette. While Dahl Pine had planned a dry veneer plant, Brooks-Willamette announced plans to expand the facility into a full-fledged plywood plant.

A site next to Brooks-Scanlon's Bend mill was selected for the particleboard plant, allowing an easy flow of shavings from the sawmill to the particleboard plant.

WVLCo. installed the German Bison system again at Bend, this one with a new wrinkle—a caulless system. (Cauls are the metal "cookie sheets" on which the board is formed.) The caulless system used a kind of screen, somewhat like a paper machine, on which the board was formed and pre-pressed. For a variety of reasons, including the fineness of the particles used at the Bend plant, the caulless system was an unmitigated disaster. John McK. Bosch, manager, remodeled the plant soon after its opening, installing a system with cauls.

Production began in March of 1966, with an annual capacity of about 35 million square feet (on a three-quarter inch basis).

II

While WVLCo. was pursuing its eastern Oregon joint venture, Santiam Lumber was looking quite another direction.

In 1964 an event occurred in a plywood plant in Arkansas that revolutionized the forest products industry. The South had once been an important lumber capital. But when the best lands were logged over, many companies closed their doors or moved on to the new frontier in the West. By 1960 a bountiful second crop was beginning to emerge. But no one was packing his tent for the South. There was one big problem: It was assumed to be impossible to make plywood out of Southern pine. There just wasn't a glue that would hold the resinous pine.

Southern universities were working to perfect a method to glue panels together. However, in 1964 a plywood making technique was developed that set the South down on its feet running.

Suddenly everyone wanted in the southern pine plywood business. From that moment on, the South was the new frontier.

Coley Wheeler and his son Sam observed the events in the South with more than a passing interest. The Wheelers could see the South as a major vehicle for Company expansion and they wanted to get in on the ground floor. Coley Wheeler, always something of a gambler at heart, was prepared to back that judgment with an investment.

In the summer of 1964 Gene Knudson and Sam Wheeler spent a great deal of time in the South looking for an opportunity. They visited their friends met through trade associations, contacted Ira Keller's paper-making friends and the local universities and Forest Service. Knudson also dropped in on an old friend, Don Burkhalter, in Ruston, Louisiana. Burkhalter was related to the James family, a prominent landowning Louisiana family with interest in the timber business.

By the time the Southern search was over, there emerged a couple of excellent possibilities. Crown Zellerbach had been negotiating with a company to construct a plywood plant in Hammond, Louisiana, near Bogalusa. Crown had extensive landholdings in the area and was willing to put up a long-term Hill-type timber supply contract to someone who would construct a plant in the heart of the timberlands. The company initially involved in the discussion had seemingly lost interest in the deal, so Crown, Knudson and Wheeler began to talk. The negotiations went well and an informal agreement was reached. But the next morning Knudson received a phone call saying that the first company had reconsidered and was going to build the plant at Hammond.

Knudson got in touch with his friend Burkhalter and he and the Wheelers began discussing a joint venture in northern Louisiana. The agreement they hammered out was to be a pattern for the Company's southern expansion. The Southern companies provided the log supply while Willamette supplied the technical know-how to operate the plants and market the product.

On November 19, 1964 the T.L. James Company and the Santiam Lumber Company formed Santiam Southern Company, a Nevada corporation. The Wheelers were reluctant to form a Louisiana corporation because roots of Louisiana law are French and difficult for an Oregon-based firm and its attorneys to grasp. Yet they didn't feel it had to be an Oregon corporation, so they chose Nevada, partly because deep down they felt the venture really was somewhat of a gamble.

Santiam Southern constructed a plywood plant in Ruston, Louisiana in 1965. The Company also purchased land north of Ruston, almost on the Arkansas border, for a green veneer plant that began running in March of 1966. Log supply in the Haynesville area was excellent, so the green veneer plant staked out a supply for the Ruston plywood plant.

In the South during that era there were no trained plywood plant workers. Henry Clark, an Oklahoman who had worked in the glue business and then became manager of the Lebanon plywood plant, went down to manage Santiam Southern. He took with him three young men from the Lebanon area who had not yet been made foremen. The day Santiam Southern opened, these were the only four workers who had been inside a plywood plant before. All the rest had to be trained from the ground up.

Clark arrived in Louisiana in February and took his first day off on Christmas Day. He had to do all the plant's maintenance work himself. Finding machine parts was a particular problem. In Oregon, where so much sawmill and plywood plant equipment is fabricated, it was easy to phone in an order for a part and have it delivered the next day. But in Louisiana, if you didn't have a part, you either rigged it up with baling wire or you shut the plant down until the part came.

It was difficult to attract qualified personnel. Plywood plants worked 7 days a week and 3 shifts a day. Sawmills in Louisiana were mostly one-shift operations and it was difficult for wood products workers to warm to the idea of swing and graveyard shifts.

Santiam and WVLCo. studied several joint ventures in the South—in Alabama, Arkansas, Florida, Texas, Georgia and Mississippi. But no further growth occurred until after the merger in 1967.

III

In the mid-60's talk of a merger of all the firms in which WVLCo. had interest began in earnest among the major stockholders of each of the firms. It had been obvious since the 50's that a merger of interests was likely. A variety of circumstances made that possibility a reality in 1967.

Probably the biggest factor in the merger was the nation's tax system. In 1966 the lumber industry was in a downturn. The price of stumpage at the beginning of the year was high, but prices for finished products during the year were low. Because a portion of the timberland owner's profit can be taxed under capital gains, this market situation resulted in a capital gains gap. In 1966 WVLCo. had more capital gains than income and therefore could have had more income subject to a reduced tax rate. Yet other companies to which WVLCo. was related were being taxed at the full corporate rate. It meant that the tax rate would have been much more favorable if the related companies merged.

A second important reason for consideration of a merger was to set the stage for offering shares for sale to the public. A merger would produce an integrated forest products firm that would be an attractive investment vehicle, resulting in improved stockholder liquidity.

The need for a centralized management for all the related firms was another important reason for the merger. Some consolidation had taken place already. In 1957 Willamette National was merged into WVLCo. While all elements were moving forward in concert, it was desirable to consolidate management for better administration and planning for future growth. A consolidated company would have more financial strength.

Yet another positive feature of the merger was for the stockholders themselves. When a stockholder died, a value had to be placed on his ownership in the Company. When shares are traded freely on the stock exchange, it's easy to establish the value of a share. It's not so easy with a closely-held company.

When the merger was finally approved, it included the Willamette Valley Lumber Co., Santiam Lumber Co., Wood Fiberboard Company (Duraflake), Western Veneer and Plywood Company and Dallas Lumber and Supply Company (two retail yards). In addition, the newly merged company exchanged shares of its stock with Western Kraft so that 80% of Western Kraft was owned by the merged firm, making Western Kraft its consolidated subsidiary.

WVLCo. brought into the merger its sawmills and plywood plants in Foster and Dallas; timber, timberlands and Hill contract; and 50 percent ownership of Brooks-Willamette.

Santiam brought its sawmill in Sweet Home; plywood plants in Lebanon, Springfield and Sweet Home; its interest in the

Hill contract; 85 percent interest in Santiam Southern, which consisted of a plywood plant in Ruston, Louisiana and a veneer plant in Haynesville, Louisiana.

The Wood Fiberboard Company added its particleboard plant, now called Duraflake Division, in Albany, Oregon.

Western Veneer and Plywood became the Griggs Division.

Dallas Lumber and Supply brought in its retail lumber yards in Dallas and Independence, Oregon.

Western Kraft had paper mills in Albany, Oregon and Richmond and Port Hueneme, California. Bag plants were located in Beaverton, Oregon and Buena Park, California. Corrugated container plants were in Beaverton; Compton and Vernon, California; Elk Grove, Aurora, Melrose Park and Rockford, Illinois; and Bellevue and Wenatchee, Washington. In addition, Western Kraft had a 33 percent interest in Druth, a 50 percent interest in WesCor and a 31.8 percent interest in Western Corrugated, Inc., with plants in Sacramento and San Leandro, California.

One of the biggest difficulties was finding a name for the new corporation. There were two schools of thought. One group felt the new name should have nothing to do with any of the elements that merged. Another felt that a combination of Willamette and Western Kraft (such as Willamette-Western) was a natural name. Most were neutral and willing to bend over backward to be sure everyone was happy with the new name. On March 3, 1967 the merger became effective and Columbia Forest Products, Inc. was born.

The name didn't really please anyone. So it was by mutual consent that the new corporation became Willamette Industries, Inc., just 17 days later on March 20th.

Directors of the new corporation were Wilson W. Clark, chairman emeritus; Coleman Wheeler, chairman; Ira Keller, vice chairman; Bill Swindells, Sr.; Bill Swindells, Jr.; Maurie Clark; Charles Curley (chairman of the board of the First Trust Company of St. Paul); Sam Davis (president of Corco); Lyman Seely (executive vice president of the First National Bank of Oregon); and Stuart Shelk (president of Ochoco Lumber).

Officers were Bill Swindells, Sr., president; Gene Knudson, executive vice president; Bill Swindells, Jr., vice president for plants and manufacturing; George Swindells, vice president for sales and marketing; Sam Wheeler, vice president for production; M.J.

Kelly, vice president for production; Marvin Coats, vice president for lands and timber; and A.R. Morgans, financial vice president and secretary-treasurer.

During its first year the new corporation had consolidated sales of over $114 million and net earnings of nearly $8.2 million.

The first major issue of Willamette Industries stock was in 1968 when Willamette registered 80,000 shares with the Securities and Exchange Commission to offer to 93 salaried employees of the company at $17 per share.

Gradually Swindells convinced the major stockholders to sell about 1 percent of their stock, thus providing a quantity of shares to be traded publicly.

In 1968, in its first full year of operation, Willamette and its subsidiaries made profits of $14.8 million on sales of $141.7 million.

CHAPTER 14

Southern Building Materials Expansion

After the initial rush into plywood making in the South, some problems began to emerge.

While the gluing processes in plywood making had been perfected, there were a few other nuances to the proper making of Southern pine plywood. Steam vats, for example were needed to condition the pine before peeling. Many Southern plants opened without these. There had been a terrific rush on equipment. Companies that couldn't wait had to settle for inferior lathes and dryers. When the market took a dip, these plants were in trouble.

Santiam Southern was not a profitable operation at first. In fact, Santiam Lumber came within a hair's breadth of selling out. But after the merger, Knudson and Sam Wheeler sat down with Henry Clark, decided what would be needed to make the plant profitable, and authorized about $500,000 in expenditures to add equipment that would put the operation in the black. It worked.

II

Sam Wheeler became vice president in charge of southern operations. One day Wheeler was visited by a young forester named John Shealy who worked for a local lumber company. Wheeler and Shealy found immediately that they could work very well together: Wheeler needed log supply for the Ruston plant and for further expansion, and Shealy knew how to get it. The Company's log procurement folks weren't doing the job and the Ruston and Haynesville plants were almost out of logs. Wheeler put Shealy on the payroll. Shealy's knowledge of area landowners proved a major factor in Willamette's ability to grow in the South.

Meanwhile, just south of Ruston, in the town of Dodson, the Hunt Lumber Company and Continental Can were involved in a joint venture called Louisiana Plywood. Hunt Lumber was a family-owned sawmill company with a timberland base.

Continental wanted out of what it considered a losing venture and offered its half for sale.

Willamette purchased Continental's 50 percent ownership in Louisiana Plywood in 1967, thereby owning half of the Dodson plywood plant. To Willamette the most important part of the deal was the timber supply contracts Continental and Hunt had signed. Through the contracts, Hunt and Continental agreed to supply the Dodson plant's projected timber supply needs for 15 years. In addition, Continental agreed to sell Santiam Southern at least 8 million board feet of peeler logs each year for 15 years. For a non-landowning company, that was a contract to celebrate.

III

The Woodard-Walker Lumber Co. was a well-known, deep-rooted Louisiana firm, formed just a couple of years before Willamette Valley Lumber Co. The Walkers and Willamette management had been friends for years. Woodard-Walker had two sawmills, in Heflin and Taylor, Louisiana and a substantial amount of timberland. In 1969 Columbia Plywood of Minden, Louisiana put its four-year-old plant on the market and Woodard-Walker-Willamette (3W) was formed to purchase it.

Woodard-Walker contracted to provide the plant's complete projected log supply for 15 years. Willamette agreed to take responsibility for sales, plant management and administration.

The 3W's opening in 1970 brought Willamette's plywood capacity in the South to just over one-quarter billion square feet annually.

IV

In 1971 Natchitoches Parish (a Louisiana Parish is a governmental unit similar to a county) found itself the reluctant owner of a four-year-old bankrupt plywood plant. In 1966 the Parish had floated a general obligation bond to build a plywood plant to attract industry. The bond issue was to be retired from lease fees paid by the operator of the plant over a 15 year period. When the market went sour in 1970, the lessee, Southply, threw in the towel. While the Parish wanted to continue to lease the plant, they discovered they would have to secure a $1.25 million federal loan for improvements to bring the plant up to date.

The Parish decided to sell. This time Willamette paired up with another long-time Louisiana lumber company with timberlands—the Martin Timber Co. In 1971 Wilmar was incorporated and offered Natchitoches Parish $625,000 for the plant. When the offer was accepted, Wilmar shelled out another $1.25 million to renovate the facility.

Again Willamette supplied the technology and the marketing capability and the Martins agreed to supply about half of the plant's log supply needs from its own timberlands and to contract for the remainder of the plant's needs.

V

In 1970 Willamette decided that raw materials were adequate in the Ruston area to support a particleboard plant. Duraflake South, Inc. was incorporated late in 1970 with Willamette owning 81% of the stock and the remaining 19% split equally between the Woodard-Walker and Hunt Lumber companies. This particleboard plant, like Willamette's other two, was to run on sawmill and plywood plant residue. Willamette felt the other companies would have more of an interest in supplying residue for the plant if they had a financial stake in the plant's operation. The plant, costing about $7 million, was completed early in 1972.

VI

Characteristically, Willamette management did not intend to live off its partners' timberlands forever. Always concerned about developing a fee timber base, John Shealy and his growing band of foresters were constantly on the look-out for timberlands to purchase. By mid-1971 the Company owned 15,000 acres in Louisiana.

In December of 1971 two large timber purchases were consummated. The Pardee family owned 52,872 acres and Davis Brothers Lumber owned 64,000 in northern Louisiana and southern Arkansas. Both of these groups approached Willamette, mainly because they had ties with Willamette's Southern partners. Willamette purchased both of the sales, retaining a total of about 70,000 acres and selling the remainder to Timber, Inc. (related to Georgia-Pacific) and to the Roy O. Martin Lumber Co.

In seven years Willamette had progressed from zero base in the South to a partner in 4 joint ventures and owner of 85,000 acres of timberland and a particleboard plant.

VII

While the expansion was rapid, it would not have been possible without Willamette's joint venture partners. They knew the South and they knew how to get things done. In turn, the Southern partners felt comfortable with Willamette's management style, its technological ability and its size. The combination was dynamite.

It was natural that the partners came to Willamette when they decided to leave the forest products industry.

In 1972 Willamette purchased the Hunt Lumber Co. with a stock transfer. Hunt owned half of the Louisiana Plywood plant at Dodson, a stud mill at Danville, sawmills at Zwolle, Columbia and Dodson, and 15,200 acres of timberland. The purchase involved 411,999 shares of Willamette's stock.

Less than two years later Wilmar was dissolved and Willamette became sole owner of the Natchitoches plywood plant.

That same year Willamette became involved in a convoluted timberland purchase. Willamette acquired timberland near Jarratt, Virginia, from Johns-Manville. Georgia-Pacific owned timberland in northern Louisiana, a portion of which had been purchased by Georgia-Pacific from Willamette when Willamette acquired the Davis and Pardee timberland. Willamette exchanged substantially all the Johns-Manville timberland for 34,000 acres of Georgia-Pacific timberland in northern Louisiana, bringing Willamette's ownership to 150,000 acres.

VIII

The most profitable use of peelable Southern pine logs was for the production of plywood rather than lumber. In 1978 the Zwolle sawmill, acquired from the Hunts, was converted into a wood processing complex that concentrated on plywood making. Today, the facility is one of the most modern and efficient in the South. A hog fuel boiler turns waste bark into energy to run the complex. A cut off saw routes saplings to the sawmill or chipper and bigger logs to the lathes for plywood making.

Peeler cores are routed to the sawmill and any material left over is routed back to the chipper to produce wood fiber for paper-making. It is a waste-free operation that can produce lumber and plywood from logs other plants consider food for the chipper.

In 1978 Willamette purchased a sawmill in Emerson, Arkansas from Continental Can. The sawmill was shut down and a wood processing complex patterned on the Zwolle concept was constructed.

Also that year a major timber purchase was consummated—Willamette acquired 21,500 acres of timberland in northern Louisiana and southern Arkansas from the Bolinger Lumber Co., Ltd. This assured a supply of timber for the Emerson complex and gave a timber supply-conscious management some breathing room.

IX

On its 75th anniversary Willamette made a purchase that brought the Company almost full circle in the South. The Woodard-Walker Lumber Co. decided to sell its half interest in 3W, their 18-month-old plywood plant in Taylor, Louisiana and 50,000 acres of timberland with mineral rights. Willamette was the successful bidder. With this land purchase, Willamette owned more timberland in the Southern pine region than in the Douglas fir region—some 250,000 acres.

From 1965 to 1980—in fifteen short years—Willamette's southern operation grew from a single joint venture in the South with no timberland to a major Southern landowner with 7 plywood plants, 4 sawmills, particleboard plant, veneer plant, paper mill and chipping plants—a fully integrated geographical operation.

CHAPTER 15

Growth and Value-Added Products

At a Fibre Box Association meeting one year, Don Pooley (president of Western Kraft) and Jack Wilson (assistant to the president) were dining with a group of corrugated container executives from other companies and the dinner talk turned to plant locations. Representatives from several large manufacturers described some of the elements their companies fed into computers to determine ideal plant locations. The men at the table turned to the two Western Kraft representatives and asked them how they decided where to build a plant. "It's simple," Pooley replied, "we just ask Ira Keller."

Indeed, it was Ira Keller's intuitive understanding of the corrugated container industry and general business principles that made Western Kraft grow so rapidly.

In the late 1960's and early 70's the game plan was expansion into Eastern and Midwestern markets. Keller's knowledge of the industry and his feel for markets were keys to this expansion.

After several difficult years at Elk Grove, the Chicago market was proving to be a good one. It was an industrial area with a high, relatively stable demand for all types of boxes. In 1967, the same year WesCor came on line, Western Kraft opened another Chicago area corrugated container plant in Aurora with a former Packaging Corporation employee at the helm, Ward Black. Start-up at Aurora was much smoother than at Elk Grove because the Company was beginning to develop personnel and experience.

That same year the long-awaited Washington state plant was constructed in Bellevue, just east of Seattle, under the direction of Dick Keller. Its progress was speeded by a fire that completely destroyed the Wenatchee sheet plant. It had the advantage of ready-made business from both Wenatchee, Wash. and Beaverton, Ore. which helped greatly with start-up.

In 1970 Western Kraft moved even further east to the Philadelphia area. Markets in Philadelphia were quite similar to those in Chicago, so management felt it could operate a profitable box plant to serve the southeast Pennsylvania-New Jersey area. Bob Connelly, a master boxmaker/salesman from the Philadelphia area, had made the decision to leave the management of Connelly Containers to his brother. Ira Keller, who had known and respected Connelly for years, saw him as the key to the Eastern market. The men met and hammered out an agreement that formed Western Kraft East, Inc., 85% owned by Western Kraft.

A plant site was purchased in an industrial park in Bellmawr, New Jersey. As the men were in a hurry to dive into the Philadelphia market, no engineering was done for the plant. The Bellmawr plant became the mirror image of the Aurora, Illinois plant.

In 1971 Western Corrugated Inc. was liquidated, and the Sacramento and San Leandro, Calif. plants became full-fledged members of the Western Kraft team.

II

The Company had no internally generated supply of linerboard for its growing Eastern and Midwestern operations. In 1970 management began looking in the South for possible paper mill locations. When Willamette made the Pardee and Davis timber purchases in 1971, Neil Duffie and consulting engineer Bill Shelton began concentrating their attention in northern Louisiana. The Company was developing a considerable manufacturing capacity in that area and held a solid base of timberland. With residuals and large tracts of private timberlands available for pulpwood purchase, northern Louisiana seemed an ideal spot.

The duo concentrated their search along the Red River in western Louisiana. Shelton recommended a location near Campti, Louisiana for the mill. After an option had been taken on property near Campti, Duffie and Shelton began visiting small towns and colleges in the area to see if there were any objections to a pulp and paper mill. Sensitized by the odor problems in Albany and local concern over start-up problems at the bleached pulp mill (which included a bomb threat to a WesCor official), Duffie and Shelton wanted to be sure the local residents had no concerns. Their visits to colleges, town officials and even an undertaker met with nothing but positive comments. One local welfare official claimed that 22% of the Parish was on food stamps and that the mill could only be considered a "God send".

A 500 acre site was purchased for the unbleached kraft linerboard mill. The mill, with a 300 ton per day capacity, was designed by Western Kraft engineers and consultants in a huge, unfinished room on the 37th floor of the First National Bank Tower in· Portland, where Willamette's headquarters had just moved. Once design work was done, key members of the engineering staff moved to Louisiana to provide on-the-spot answers to construction questions. Eddie Mahan was in charge of field work.

The mill was completed under budget in 1974 and employees were lured from both Albany and Hawesville to fill many jobs. The state of Louisiana provided vocational training to local folks so they could take the semi-skilled positions. Tim Campbell was brought in from Elk Grove as resident manager.

When the $25 million plant was up to its rated capacity, it increased the Company's paper production capacity by 30%. Expansions were soon underway and continued through 1978. (Capacity had been expanded to 840 tons per day by 1980.)

III

With a bag and several box plants in the Los Angeles area, the Company was becoming a recognized name in packaging. Ira Keller had felt for a long time that a folding carton manufacturing facility would round out capabilities in southern California. A folding carton plant could enhance the Company's packaging reputation, provide another product for corrugated container customers and could itself create corrugated and, indirectly, linerboard customers.

In December 1967 Western Kraft purchased Flintkote's Vernon, California folding carton plant. A new, modern plant was constructed in an orange grove near Camarillo (between Los Angeles and Santa Barbara) in 1969 and Jack Moers, formerly sales manager, was promoted to general manager.

IV

Over the years the two Kalof corrugated container plants in Vernon, California—Quaker and Hand—were merged into one plant called the Vernon Division. That plant was no prize. It was a wood frame and sheet metal building that had enough holes to give pigeons free access to the plant.

There was opportunity for increased corrugated sales in the Los Angeles area. Management had to decide whether to drop the Vernon facility entirely or to continue it and construct another moderate-sized plant. They decided to build a showplace and close Vernon. In 1974 a new and completely modern plant was constructed in Cerritos, a unique 300,000 square foot facility with plenty of room. It remains today the Company's biggest container plant in square footage, with spacious offices and a formal dining room for entertaining customers.

While the neighboring Compton plant under management of Dan Small was designed with agricultural and industrial customers in mind, the Cerritos plant, under Jack Jefferies, went after customers that needed value-added specialty boxes.

Completion of the Cerritos plant and acquisition of the folding carton plant gave the Company a strong base in southern California.

V

By the mid-1970's Campti had expanded its capacity to 400 tons per day and had located wood fiber in eastern Texas that could help the mill expand to 700 tons per day to make better use of the capital investment. That meant, however, that a market, preferably an internal one, had to be found to fuel the intended expansion.

For a long time management had hoped Sam Davis might be interested in merging Corco (which consisted of five container plants and half ownership of WesCor) into Willamette. At this point, however, he showed no inclination to do so. Management began to look for opportunities for acquisition of corrugated container plants and sites for construction of a new facility.

Two areas in the South looked attractive for expansion: Dallas and Atlanta. Atlanta had been hit by a recession more severely than Dallas and two new corrugated container plants had been built recently in Atlanta. So management began to zero in on the Dallas-Ft. Worth area.

In the meantime, Potlatch had decided to sell its container plants near Pittsburgh, Pennsylvania and Riegelsville, New Jersey. The plants were old but the price was right—both could be purchased from Potlatch for the price engineers were kicking around for constructing a new plant in Dallas. After careful study of both plants, management felt it could make a go of running the Potlatch operations and purchased them in 1975. Bob Connelly eventually took over the management of the Riegelsville plant and turned it into a very profitable operation that branched out into value-added specialty items like labeled and die cut boxes.

Pittsburgh, on the other hand, proved a much greater challenge. A variety of managers tried their hands at the Pittsburgh operation. Eventually, they built business and had a profit for several months. But a lengthy strike put the plant back in the red. By that time Corco, which had plants in the same general area, had merged with Willamette, and volume of linerboard use was not so critical. The plant was closed in 1979 and the building and equipment sold.

A site between Dallas and Ft. Worth, in Grand Prairie, Texas, was chosen for the construction of a new corrugated container plant which opened in February 1976. Bill Kinnune personally directed the construction of the plant and supervised its start-up. Experienced Company people from all over the nation were brought in to man the plant. It was a very successful start-up.

Later that year Sam Davis contacted the Company about the acquisition of Corco, Inc.

The Company jumped at the chance. Management could see great economies in getting both the Kentucky paper mills under one ownership. Corco's corrugated container plants in Delaware, Ohio; Huntington, West Virginia; Bowling Green, Kentucky; Muncie, Indiana and Grand Rapids, Michigan (a sheet plant) were attractive.

Corco also owned a plastics company, Liqui-box and wanted to retain these operations. In order to work out the complex transaction, Liqui-box was spun off to Corco shareholders, after which Willamette Industries stock was exchanged for Corco stock, making Corco a 100% owned Willamette subsidiary.

In 1979 the Company closed a marketing gap on the West Coast by constructing a container plant in eastern Washington at Moses Lake to meet the needs of local food processors.

VI

The geographic growth of the corrugated container division was only a part of the story. Keller had developed a cadre of men with excellent management abilities. Out in the "field" were dozens of men who could take management's decisions and parlay them into successful operations. Men like Bill Kinnune, Kirby Hall, Leo Dozoretz, Bob Hogeboom, John Plunkett, Ward Black, and Rudy Gingg were among the leaders who developed the corrugated division.

Under the direction of these men container plants were expanded and modernized frequently to keep pace with the latest container-making techniques. There has never been a research and development department in the corrugated container division. But each container plant has developed an unusually close relationship with its customers—a relationship that has led to some significant container developments.

For example, in the mid-60's Mattel was purchasing boxes from the Vernon plant and placing lithographed labels on them in their own plant. The toy manufacturer wanted the strength of corrugated to protect its toys, yet needed a colorful label for the box for point-of-purchase appeal. Mattel ran the labels through a gluer, then assembly-line workers attached the label to the box. It was a tedious, expensive process. Mattel asked the Cerritos staff if the procedure could be improved.

Jack Jeffries and Bob Morrison started investigating the possibilities in 1964. In 1967 a first prototype began running labeled boxes. Cannibalizing equipment from other industries, the men put together a piece of machinery that could apply a full-color label to a box. That invention was followed by an improved model that could accept bigger boxes. Then a third prototype was produced that could print two colors, die cut and label. The machine is unique in the industry.

The Compton plant, with the help of Tim Milligan, improved the wax dip process by automating the loading and unloading function for the first time in response to its agricultural customers' desire for lower-cost boxes.

Automatic corrugated stackers, which took the worst job—unloading sheets from the corrugator—out of the plant, were developed and tested in the Sacramento plant. The Sacramento stacker was the first low-cost, high speed off-bearing system on the market.

Working with customers to produce a design to meet their needs led to some exciting innovations. Work with celery and asparagus growers produced new types of containers, replacing wooden crates. Consultation with the wine industry resulted in a patented 18 liter wine box. Corco had several patents, mostly on bulk bins, that were acquired by Western Kraft in the merger. These added a new dimension to the corrugated container line.

The Delaware, Ohio design lab has a certified safe transit testing lab. That lab has produced transit-safe boxes for industrial customers and has even helped customers improve their products to withstand operational and shipping stress.

Creativity in design, production and sales have been encouraged in part by each plant's autonomy.

VII

That same philosophy was responsible for the well-managed growth of the bag division. By the late 60's a significant portion of the West Coast bag market had been captured by the division's two West Coast plants. Future growth for the division would have to be in other geographic areas.

In 1976 the bag division expanded into the Dallas-Ft. Worth market by installing bag machines in the Dallas-Ft. Worth corrugated plant. (The division later constructed its own plant and began production there in 1979.) Together, the three bag plants worked on sales strategy to attract and keep customers. The bag division's sales force began to develop a series of on-the-bag promotional campaigns. One campaign, bags printed with tornado and hurricane information, won the National Weather Service's Public Service Award.

In 1973 Chuck Carlbom, in charge of the bag division, opened the Company's first ink plant in Beaverton for the in-house production of ink for bag and box printing. Adhesives were soon added to the plant's product line and a facility to serve the Eastern plants was added at Delaware, Ohio in 1978.

In 1979, after intensive investigation of the role of plastics in the bag market, the Company purchased equipment, installed it in a leased facility and began offering high-density, polyethylene bags as an adjunct to its paper bag line.

VIII

In 1969 Willamette began its first paper venture outside of the packaging industry.

Dick Keller had been watching the business forms market for some time and was convinced it was the biggest paper growth market available. In 1969 a small pilot plant was opened in Beaverton.

When the plant opened it didn't have a specialty. Keller was still feeling out the market, trying to determine what the plant's philosophy should be. Keller soon decided the plant should specialize in producing long-run continuous forms. Bill Detwiler joined the plant to help carry out that goal.

The policy proved a profitable one. The long-run continuous computer forms market generated tons of orders and kept the plant running almost non-stop. In addition, the continuous computer forms market was growing at a dynamic clip—faster than the average of the industry and faster than the economy as a whole.

At first Willamette had some difficulty breaking into the forms market. The Company's competitors called its salesmen "the loggers" and warned customers tempted to switch to the Willamette brand to stick to professional forms makers. The sales staff under Ron Stover worked hard to establish Company identity.

In 1974 Keller felt the division should expand into the Eastern market. A man with vast experience in the forms market, Ken Hopkins, was hired to open a forms plant in Langhorne, Pennsylvania, in 1975, following the same marketing philosophy as the Beaverton plant.

From the beginning, almost all sales of business forms were done by Company salesmen with only a small amount sold through brokers to very small users. Over the years, Willamette developed a system of satellite sales offices and distribution centers throughout the East and West to be able to supply customers with stock computer forms within a few hours' notice.

The Langhorne sales organization moved westward, setting up sales offices and warehouses in Pennsylvania, Ohio and Indiana. Customers from these sales areas provided a customer base for the Indianapolis forms plant when it opened in 1979. The Indianapolis plant began cultivating customers along the Mississippi that will serve as a customer base for the Dallas-Ft. Worth plant when it opens in 1981. A similar sales and distribution center arrangement helped build customers for the Cerritos, California plant which opened in 1980.

For years one selling tool was Willamette's bleached pulp capacity and its Tennessee Timberlands. While Willamette did not make business forms paper, it did grow trees and make the raw material for making forms bond. Many customers felt this raw material production and manufacturing capability would give Willamette an edge in times of paper shortages. The majority of forms makers have no timber growing or papermaking capacity.

But in 1980 Willamette took a step to bring this maverick division into the fold—it announced plans to add a paper machine to the bleached pulp mill near Hawesville, Kentucky to make business forms paper. The vertical integration that had been a success in Willamette's other operations was finally to be a part of the forms division's productive future. (Behind the mill's ability to expand was the Corco merger. Bringing the medium mill and the bleached pulp mill together under one ownership had allowed pulp and paper vice president Steve Rogel and general manager Marion Holt to integrate the systems at the two mills at attractive cost savings.)

This announcement of the new forms bond paper machine put Willamette in an enviable position in the business forms industry—it made the Company a business forms maker that controlled production from growth of the tree to stacking in the customer's storeroom, giving Willamette total control over quality.

IX

Growth for the Building Materials Group after the merger was spectacular in the South, as illustrated in Chapter 14; and measured and calculated in the West.

While many of Willamette's Western mills were old, the Company continually maintained and modernized facilities to take advantage of the most recent developments in automation and research. Men like Lyle Dragoo and Al Trom worked to keep the Company's older mills at peak efficiency.

In addition to updating older operations, Willamette was able to take advantage of acquisitions as they became available. In 1972 Rex Clemens decided to leave the forest products business. Clemens had a green veneer operation in Philomath, Oregon, about six miles west of Corvallis, and 19,500 acres of timberland. Willamette purchased his holdings which are now the Company's Philomath veneer plant and its Alsea Tree Farm.

In 1974 opportunity again knocked. William Bauman was a man after Willamette's own heart. In 1946 he and his Dad had built a portable sawmill in the Sweet Home area. He had no timberlands and no capital to purchase any. He later bought a planing mill outside Lebanon to which he added a sawmill that became his principal operation. Because he had no timberlands, he began to specialize in sawing cull logs. He'd buy cull logs and spinouts from plywood lathes—fiber other companies thought fit only for the chipper—and convert them into valuable products.

Bauman developed specialty markets for much of this low-grade lumber in the mining and transportation industries. His mill was a major supplier of chips for the Albany paper mill.

In 1974 Bauman purchased Lebanon Lumber Company, Indianola Wood Products, the Lebanon Machine Company and WJH, Inc., a trucking company. Marvin Coats helped put a deal together that sold the entire package to Willamette. Today the Bauman mill continues to make lumber, Indianola converts cull logs to lumber and chips, Lebanon Lumber makes peeler cores into studs and chips, Lebanon Machine fabricates sawmill and plywood plant equipment for Willamette and other companies and Lebanon Trucking hauls the Company's wood products.

X

The value-added concept of growth was not limited to the Paper Group. The Building Materials Group developed several value-added product lines in the mid-1970's.

As the cost of solid wood began to increase, furniture and cabinet makers became major consumers of plywood and particleboard. They'd buy carloads of these materials and cut them to size. It was often a wasteful operation. The purchaser would have to pay freight on material that would eventually become waste at his plant. These operations, sometimes located in inner cities, had difficulty disposing of the waste. The answer was to custom-cut plywood and particleboard into the needed parts and ship them east for assembly. All three of Willamette's particleboard plants could do custom cutting to some extent. The Company decided to carry the concept further with a custom cutting plant that could eliminate the need for cutting, routing and drilling equipment at the customer's assembly site.

The Custom Products Division was opened in Albany in 1972.

A similar idea led to the purchase of Mobol Products in Wilsonville, Oregon, by Brooks-Willamette in 1975. A major user of particleboard for the manufacture of grain-printed drawer sides, Mobol was selling out because of marketing difficulties.

Brooks-Willamette purchased Mobol to protect a market and because they believed in the potential of the drawer side business. (Mobol and Custom Products were merged in 1977 after Willamette and Brooks-Scanlon divided the interests of Brooks-Willamette. Willamette kept the particleboard plant in Bend—KorPINE—and Mobol Products. Brooks-Scanlon kept the Redmond plywood plant and sawmill.)

A third logical move into the value-added area was the expansion of the retail division. Willamette had always sold lumber at retail. In the early days farmers and townsfolk went directly to the sawmill to buy lumber for building.

In the 20's and 30's the concept expanded so that customers could buy more than just lumber. The retail outlet installed at Foster could provide everything needed to construct a home—lumber, nails, roofing, gutter stock, etc. These outlets were gradually phased out as independent businesses in each community began to prosper. At the time of the merger, Willamette Industries had only two retail outlets—at Dallas and Independence.

But George Swindells was convinced that a retail chain could work for Willamette. It was something that could be done without an expanded resource base, it related to primary lines of business and it would help production and sales people keep their finger on the pulse of consumer trends.

Willamette leased the Garrigus chain of retail stores in 1974, with stores in McMinnville, Newberg, Lincoln City, Forest Grove and Sherwood, Oregon. Later the Independence and Sherwood stores were closed. Other outlets were acquired in Tigard and The Dalles, Oregon and Vancouver, Washington.

A fourth value-added line was developed at the Company's three particleboard plants. In 1965 the Duraflake plant installed its first paint line to fill and prime particleboard to increase its value to manufacturers. Duraflake HMC (hot melt coat) was developed to coat particleboard with a wax for applications around food or in damp areas. In 1975 Duraflake FR, developed by Y.C. Cheo, earned a class 1 flame spreading rating through testing done by Underwriter's Laboratories. In 1980 this was the only fire-rated particleboard produced in the United States.

KorPINE at Bend added its second line in 1969. A paint line was installed in 1973 and four years later, a revolutionary new electron beam curing system was installed in the plant. Called Kor-Tron EB, the new board is coated with acrylic which is bombarded with a beam of accelerated electrons that quickly cure the paint. The board, which comes in any color of the rainbow or wood grain prints, made strong inroads during the Company's anniversary year into markets previously occupied by high-pressure laminates. Suitable for all vertical surfaces and low-wear horizontal surfaces, the board performs many of the functions of a high pressure laminate at a fraction of the cost.

A paint line was installed at Duraflake South in 1980, adding value to the plant's Southern pine particleboard, SurePine.

Willamette's trend towards value-added products has been an extension of its goal of making the most of the best—increasing profit per unit while maintaining the Company's raw material demand at a constant level.

During 1980, a ceremony was held to note the expansion of the bleached pulp mill to include the production of forms paper. Governor John Y. Brown, Judge Jim Fallin and Willamette Vice Chairman Neil Duffie, bolted down a steel I beam at the celebration.

Bill Swindells and Louisiana Governor Edwin Edwards break ground for the Red River linerboard mill at Campti, November, 1972.

CHAPTER 16

Intensive Management in the Timberlands

Today foresters have developed a way to get more fiber without purchasing additional land: Intensive management.

The intensive management techniques practiced today —thinning, fertilizing, weed control, genetic improvement and careful preparation of the planting site—were not commonplace until the 1960's.

When stumpage was worth only a few dollars a thousand board feet, intensive management was a poor investment. Forest land management during that era meant insuring that the land could reforest naturally and protecting the resulting young stand from fire.

With stumpage selling at low prices, landowners could wait for Nature to restock the lands. In that era WVLCo. foresters would do stocking surveys during the third year after harvest to be sure the land was growing its full contingent of trees. If not, seedlings would be hand-planted as time and money allowed.

Once stumpage reached about $50 per thousand board feet in the late 1960's, intensive forest management became serious business. A landowner could no longer afford to have his land idle and he could no longer afford not to hand plant, thin, fertilize and prepare the ground for a new crop. By the mid-60's Willamette was using all the modern-day forest management techniques on its tree farms. In fact, Willamette undertook the first fertilization project in the Douglas fir region.

II

The Company's forestry staff in Oregon expanded from 1 to 31, and the tree farms were divided into logical management units under timberlands manager Morris Bergman. Resident tree farm managers like Graydon Adcock, John Timm, Norm Marsh, Bob McNitt, Bob Berends, Dan Upton and Leroy Volz undertook practices that brought all of Willamette's Western tree farms under intensive management.

The scientific planning of roads to provide the maximum access with minimum removal of land from the timberland base has been accomplished by engineers like Claude Willows and Art Moser.

On-the-ground supervision of harvest operations—to maintain forest values during harvest—has been another critical feature of the Company's management program. Men like Larry Christiansen, Rex Pemberton and Dutch LeFors have lent their capable supervision to harvest operations.

III

The Company's Louisiana, Arkansas and Texas timberlands are managed by a staff of 28 professional foresters under the direction of Carroll Cochran and Johnny Spears. While the terrain, shorter rotation cycle and weather conditions dictate different types of intensive management techniques, the goal of management in the South is the same as in the Douglas fir region: Produce as much fiber as possible per acre in perpetuity.

Mineral rights on Willamette's Southern timberlands have become more and more significant yearly. According to Louisiana law a landowner may keep mineral rights after selling his land. If after ten years minerals have not been found or exploration has not begun, the mineral rights pass to the new owner. Willamette purchased some lands with mineral rights and continues to accrue rights on other lands yearly. Natural gas is abundant in the northern Louisiana area and there are several wells on Company timberlands. Lignite, a low-grade coal, is also found on Company timberlands and may someday play a significant role in the nation's energy picture.

Exploration, drilling and pipelines often take small areas of the timberlands out of production. In order to make use of these areas as well as powerline and road rights-of-way, the Company has hired a full-time wildlife biologist to supervise the planting of these areas to food plots for game animals. This program has made good use of otherwise unproductive land while successfully re-establishing wild turkey flocks and increasing the deer and game bird populations in the area.

As Willamette's Southern timberlands are inter-mixed with many small woodlots, the Louisiana foresters offer a landowner assistance program to their neighbors. In this program, Willamette's foresters provide small landowners with technical assistance to help them manage their timberlands. In return for this service, the foresters ask only the right to make an offer for the landowner's trees when he decides to harvest.

IV

Willamette's 84,000 acres in Tennessee contain principally hardwoods. These lands are managed by Mayford Williams and one other forester. Mature timber is selectively harvested and sold to local sawmills specializing in items like railroad ties, flooring and pallet materials. Chips from these operations are shipped to the Kentucky paper mills.

The foresters' current management program consists of converting the poorer hardwood sites, or about one-third of the Company's land, to loblolly pine. This will make the most productive use of the Tennessee Timberlands while improving the quality of the remaining hardwood timber.

V

By 1980 Willamette's nationwide holdings were 555,000 acres and intensive management practices were carried out on one-eighth of the Company's forest lands each year, a remarkably high figure for any forest landowner.

Willamette's outstanding record in forest management could be attributed primarily to one person: Gene Knudson. In the mid-50's Knudson became logging and timberlands manager for the Company, then moved on to vice president and later president. When Bill Swindells retired, Knudson became chairman of the board. A forester convinced of the success of intensive management and the renewability of the crop, Knudson always saw that intensive management programs received their fair share of the Company's annual budget.

His faith in intensive management is borne out by the healthy, thrifty stands growing on Willamette's tree farms today.

VI

While the main purpose of Willamette's timberlands has always been the growth of commercial timber, other uses have been encouraged. Firewood cutting permits are available free on all tree farms, their frequency of use escalated by the energy crisis.

Hunting, fishing and hiking have always been encouraged. Formal programs of wildlife management for tree farms are available in the states of Tennessee and Louisiana, and Willamette participates in these programs.

Willamette has never attempted to manage developed recreation areas on its tree farms, preferring to donate such sites to appropriate organizations. When Willamette purchased the Metzger timberlands in Oregon, which included Rainbow Lake (with cabins, a bath house, boat house, trout-stocked lake, boat landing, swimming facilities and a lodge), the Company donated the areas to Yamhill County for a youth park and juvenile rehabilitation center. Similarly, a lodge, bunkhouse and 138 acres at the headwaters of the Nestucca River in Oregon were donated to the Cascade Area Council of the Boy Scouts. Two sites in Lane County, Oregon and two in Polk County (including the George T. Gerlinger Park near Black Rock) have been donated to counties for park use.

With the exception of certain areas where logging is in progress, all of Willamette's timberlands are open to the public.

VII

When Louis Gerlinger, Sr. bought his first timberlands in Polk County in 1901, he had intended to build a railroad, log the lands and sell stump ranches to homesteaders. Those lands never saw a plow.

The Black Rock lands Gerlinger first logged with misery whips and steam donkies are now producing a second crop—ultimate testimony to the renewability of the resource.

In the year of its 75th anniversary celebration, 1980, the Company Gerlinger founded was a sustained-yield operation—able to provide a substantial portion of its own timber supply needs indefinitely. In fact, Company foresters had been holding back a bit on harvest, leaving the Company with a healthy savings account of timber to help offset the projected shortfall of mature timber on Oregon's private forest lands until the year 2000.

CHAPTER 17

Willamette's People and Philosophies

After the merger, Western Kraft was a subsidiary of Willamette Industries, managed as a separate entity with its own chairman of the board and president, Ira Keller.

Keller had not really wanted a full time job when he signed on with Western Kraft. He'd made a deal with Swindells that he would only spend about half of his time working on the development of Western Kraft; the remainder he wanted to devote to civic and personal pursuits.

At first he hadn't taken the time he had intended. But as he began to develop a cadre of men with excellent management potential, he turned more of the responsibility over to them. Keller was an aggressive, enthusiastic, people-oriented person who seemed to attract men with the same qualities. He put together a powerful team.

In 1969 Keller decided to turn over the reins of day-to-day management of the Company. The logical choice was to his two first lieutenants, Neil Duffie, vice president of manufacturing, and Don Pooley, vice president of sales. When Keller relinquished the job of president to become chairman of the board of Western Kraft in 1969, he made Neil Duffie vice chairman and Don Pooley president. When Keller retired completely in 1972, Duffie became chairman of the board and chief executive officer of Western Kraft.

In December of 1970 Willamette purchased the remaining minority interest in Western Kraft, making it a wholly-owned subsidiary.

In February of 1971 Coley Wheeler retired as chairman of the board of Willamette, Bill Swindells was named chairman and chief executive officer, and Gene Knudson became president.

When the Western Kraft Paper Group became an operating division of Willamette in 1974, management of the two divisions began to merge. That year Bill Swindells was chairman; Gene Knudson, president and chief executive officer; Bill Knodell, financial vice president and secretary-treasurer; Neil Duffie and Bill

Swindells, Jr., executive vice presidents; and Marvin Coats and Don Pooley, vice presidents. Leo Dozoretz, Dick Keller, Rudy Gingg, Bill Paxson and George Swindells were division vice presidents.

When Bill Swindells retired in 1976, Knudson took over as chairman and chief executive officer; Duffie as president and chief operations officer. In 1980, in preparation for Knudson's retirement, Duffie became vice chairman and Bill Swindells, Jr., president and chief operations officer.

The Board of Directors during the Company's anniversary year included Maurie Clark (vice chairman of the board of Rollins, Burdick, Hunter of Oregon, Inc.), Neil Duffie (vice chairman of Willamette), E.B. Hart (president and chief executive officer of Payless Drugstores Northwest), Dick Keller (president of Keller Enterprises, Inc.), Gene Knudson (chairman of the board and chief executive officer of Willamette), Charles Kuhn (rancher and investor), Louis Perry (president of Standard Insurance Company), Lyman Seely (vice chairman of the board of First National Bank of Oregon), Bill Swindells, Jr. (president and chief operations officer of Willamette), and Sam Wheeler (vice president, Barclay Logging Co.).

Officers in addition to Knudson, Duffie and Swindells, Jr. were Felix Hammack, Bill Knodell, Don Pooley and Bill Shields, executive vice presidents of the corporation; Marvin Coats, vice president and senior vice president of the Building Materials Group; Bill Paxson, vice president; Jerry Parsons, controller. Paper Group officers included: Bill Kinnune, executive vice president; Leo Dozoretz, senior vice president; Chuck Carlbom, Ken Hopkins, Mick Onustock and Steve Rogel, vice presidents. Building Materials Group officers were: Dick Davis, John Shealy and Floyd Vike, vice presidents.

II

In addition to developing its top management, Willamette worked to develop management at all levels. Its Earn and Learn Scholarship Program, developed by Bill Paxson, has recruited young, energetic cream-of-the-crop talents in the fields of forestry, forest products, engineering and business for many years.

While salaried level turn-over in the Company is extremely low, young managers have had an opportunity for rapid advancement through the Company's growth. A consistent policy of promotion from within has given talented production and sales managers room for growth. For example, at age 30 Bill Shields joined Willamette as a plywood salesman, manning a phone in the Albany, Oregon office. Soon he had the opportunity to move into production in the West, then the South. He became vice president in charge of the Southern operations and by the age of 43 was executive vice president in charge of the Company's building materials operations. Bill Kinnune, who joined the Company as a corrugated container salesman, moved rapidly up the ladder in sales and production positions to become executive vice president in charge of the entire corrugated container division at the age of 41.

One area of limited growth, however, has been in actual administration. Willamette has always been considered a lean organization because of its lack of corporate staff. A bare-bones headquarters staff does accounting, computer programming and engineering. Willamette's overhead in 1980 was only 5.6% of sales, one of the lowest in the industry.

III

The corporation began to concern itself about its image in the investment community soon after the merger. Management commissioned a noted Portland graphic designer, Doug Lynch, to develop Willamette's now-familiar logo. The center of the logo represents a seedling and the abstract 5-sided form surrounding the seedling represents the concept of packaging.

Wishing to expand its geographic base for stockholders, Willamette began a program of financial relations under the direction of Bill Knodell, who took over as chief financial officer and secretary-treasurer after A.R. Morgans retired in 1971. Management began to put on programs for financial analysts' societies across the United States. Subsequent articles in the business and trade press spoke of Willamette Industries as an up-and-coming new force in the forest products industry. A *Wall Street Journal* and *Barron's* ad campaign in the late 1970's added to Willamette's increasing name familiarity in the East.

In 1973 81% of Willamette's shares of stock were owned in 5 Western states. By 1980 the Willamette name was well known in the Eastern financial community and ownership in those 5 states had been reduced to 69%.

The corporation moved to new headquarters on the 38th floor of the First National Bank Tower in October 1972. Being on the top floor of Portland's highest building seemed appropriate to the Company's growing prestige.

IV

Throughout Willamette's 75 years, the concepts that developed the Company have remained intact. While the Company has changed dramatically, the lessons taught by history have been retained. As Knudson wrote in 1979:

> Simply defined, the Company abides by conservative financial standards which enable it to take advantage of opportunities which arise. These opportunities (whether acquisition, revision or expansion) must benefit our shareholders, must not be of a size to entail extraordinary risk, and must relate to our business expertise.
>
> Basic to this particular business is raw material, its utilization and integrated manufacture and marketing. Along the way, we must squeeze out as many dollars as possible by efficient operations, value-added items and innovative marketing. The raw material base has always been restrictive from an availability and cost standpoint and probably will continue to be so for the foreseeable future. Many plants have been closed or modified to maximize overall return from available resources. Others have not increased in size but have grown in return by adding more sophisticated products and processes . . .
>
> We must be alert for opportunities and I am sure many will come along which fit our requirements for reasonably secure raw materials, and most profitable conversion in

our lines of business. I see nothing on the horizon which would indicate a stagnation of profit growth for the company over reasonably short periods of time.

Knudson defined the Company's basic policies of operation and growth very simply to the Los Angeles Analyst Society that same year:

1. Fully utilize the forest resource;
2. Operate plants continuously and efficiently;
3. Provide stable employment, thereby maintaining a skilled workforce;
4. Service our customers reliably with quality products;
5. Expand only to benefit shareholders;
6. Stay in lines of business we know;
7. Stay in domestic operations as long as opportunities exist;
8. Adhere to conservative financial policies, relying largely on internally-generated funds for expansion.

Balance has perhaps been the key to growth. Willamette's ability to keep all elements in balance—timberlands, primary processing and converting facilities—has made it a stable performer.

The balance between building materials and paper products has kept the Company on an even keel despite market conditions. Historically, markets for building materials and paper products have proven counter-cyclical. When paper product sales begin to drag, housing starts perk up, and vice versa.

Willamette also has kept a good balance between raw material supply and finished product. Management's constant efforts to increase its fee timber base have proven wise. In the decade of the 1970's Willamette purchased close to one-quarter million acres of timberland. In 1980 the Company could provide, through fee timberlands and long-term contracts, just over 50% of its saw log needs. This controlled supply of fee timber has allowed flexibility in meeting plant requirements in spite of fluctuating availability from other sources.

People like John Davis, western manager of logging and timberlands, have continued Gerlinger's involvement in government decisions affecting timber supply by taking an active role in industry committees.

V

Longevity in corporations is indeed a badge of success. The depressions, recessions and technological changes in the history of the forest products industry have left many companies as only memories. Through a combination of factors, including good management, dedicated employees and a whole lot of luck, Willamette has survived.

Willamette's corporate history represents more than just a collection of fires, court battles and partnerships. It serves as a foundation to the present; a signpost to the future.

In the late 1920's, when Gerlinger ordered the destruction of the Dallas sawmill's wigwam burner and the construction of a chip mill, he undoubtedly thought them small economies that made good business sense. And indeed they did. One led to the Company's current 68% energy self-sufficiency; the other to the establishment of the nation's first paper mill to rely totally on residuals from the building materials industry for its raw material supply.

The Company's fight for the use of cull logs in plywood making, the purchase of Bill Bauman's fiber efficient mills, the start-up of Port Hueneme, the entry into value-added products—all of these moves were more than just history. They represent a base, a solid foundation on which Willamette's future will be built. As energy prices skyrocket, Willamette's self-sufficiency will place it in an extremely competitive position as others play catch-up. Its concentration on residuals and on efficient operations making the most of available raw materials will hold it in good stead in a fiber-short future. Its development of value-added enterprises and its creative marketing strategy will allow expansion of profits without a need to expand its raw materials base. Its compact vertical integration will help to keep quality high while holding the line on raw material costs. Its concentration on two lines of business will enable it to make the most of growth opportunities. Its manageable size and lack of corporate bureaucracy will give it superior mobility.

The combination of making the most of raw materials, business opportunities and people's talents has been an astounding success. On its 75th anniversary year, 1980, Willamette had net earnings of $63.3 million on sales of $940 million, closing in on the benchmark of $1 billion in sales. Total assets of the corporation were $802 million. Its 8,530 employees worked in 60 manufacturing facilities in 14 states. Its holdings included 555,000 acres of timberlands in Oregon, Louisiana, Arkansas, Texas and Tennessee. That single sawmill in Dallas, Oregon had truly blossomed into an integrated forest products company.

This is not the closing chapter of Willamette Industries' corporate story. It is rather a convenient viewing point on the way to 100 years of making the most of the best.

William Paxson, Gene Knudson, C.R. Duffie, C.W. Knodell

William Shields, William Swindells, Jr., D.B. Pooley, Felix Hammack

Richard Davis, Floyd Vike, John Shealy, Marvin Coats

Kenneth Hopkins, Michael Onustock, Steven Rogel

Leo Dozoretz, William Kinnune, Charles Carlbom

Maurie D. Clark
Vice Chairman of
the Board
Rollins Burdick
Hunter of Oregon, Inc.,
Insurance Brokers;
Portland

Ed Hart
President and Chief
Executive Officer
Payless Drug Stores
Northwest,
Portland

Richard B. Keller
President
Keller Enterprises,
Portland

Charles B. Kuhn
Rancher and
businessman
San Jose, California

Louis B. Perry
President and Director
Standard Insurance
Company,
Portland

Lyman E. Seely
Vice Chairman of
the Board
First Interstate Bank
of Oregon, Portland

Samuel C. Wheeler
Vice President
Barclay Logging
Company, Portland

Board of Directors (non-officers)

WILLAMETTE INDUSTRIES' DATELINE

1901 / October- November	Gerlinger purchases 7,000 acres for railroad right-of-way in Polk County. Salem, Falls City & Western Railway incorporated.
1903 / May 29	Dallas-Falls City portion of Salem, Falls City and Western completed.
1905 / July	George Gerlinger and others begin operating Falls City Lumber Co.
December	George Cone builds Cone Lumber Co. on terminal grounds of Salem, Falls City & Western.
1906 / March 3	Willamette Valley Lumber Co. agrees to buy Cone Lumber Co.
March	Railroad completed to Black Rock.
1908 / August	Salem, Falls City & Western railway begins extension toward Salem.
1912 / August	Salem, Falls City & Western railway sold.
1917 / August 10	Balderee Camp fire.
December	Loyal Legion of Loggers and Lumbermen chapter formed at Willamette Valley Lumber Co.
1919	Gerlinger appointed to the State Board of Forestry.
1920	O.M. Clark and W.W. Clark purchase Pittock's share of WVLCo.
July 10	Sawmill burned completely.
1922	Fire destroys 100,000 ft. finished lumber.
1923 / October 4	WVLCo. purchases first O&C stumpage.

1924	Fire destroys logging camp.
	Fire destroys planer, dry kilns, finished lumber.
1926	"The General" with Buster Keaton filmed at Black Rock.
1927 / January	WVLCo. installs first commercial chipper operation.
1929	WVLCo. tears down wigwam burner.
1933 / December	Federal District Court hears WVLCo.'s request for injunction on Labor Code enforcement.
1934	Mill G opens (closed in 1950).
1935 / January	Gerlingers and Swindells buy Corvallis Lumber Co. (closed 1955).
1938 / December	Hammond Lumber lands purchased. (9,745 acres).
1939	Wright-Blodgett lands purchased (3,880 acres).
July 28	Logging starts at Snow Peak.
1940 / October 10	Fire destroys planer, drying sheds, shipping sheds, 10 million feet of lumber and cut-up plant. Damage over $500,000.
1941	AFL Local 2714 started at Dallas mill.
1943	Snow Peak & Black Rock lands officially designated "Tree Farms."
September 21	Army-Navy E Award presented at Dallas.
December	Railroad operations above Black Rock close permanently.
1944 / March	Second Army-Navy E Award presented.
May	6-day strike; WVLCo.'s first.
1945	Dallas Lumber & Supply Co. formed (closed 1961).
July 16	Beginning of fire above Black Rock. 13,000 acres burned.

1946 / February	Hill contract signed.
February	Willamette National incorporated.
1947 / May 23	Sawmill operations begin at Willamette National (Foster) (closed June 1968).
1948 / October	George Gerlinger dies.
	Independence Lumber Yard purchased (closed 1975).
1950	Woods operations install first radios.
1951 / December	WVLCo. purchases interest in Santiam Lumber.
1952	First major purchase of cut-over lands.
1953 / December	Western Veneer & Plywood (Griggs Div.) purchased by WVLCo. and Santiam.
1954 / October 21	Western Kraft Corporation formed.
1955 / August 15	Plywood plant constructed in Dallas, (Ore.)
	Roaring River Tree Farm purchased (7,000).
July	San Leandro, Calif. corrugated container plant constructed.
September	Western Kraft Albany paper mill begins production.
October	State of Oregon dedicates 1,000 acre George T. Gerlinger State Experimental Forest.
1956	Fischer (Marcola) lands purchased (21,966 acres).
	Yakima, Wash. corrugated sales office opens.
October	Beaverton, Ore. corrugated container plant opens.
1957 / April	Carlton Sawmill (LHL) purchased (closed 1961) Trask Mt. Tree Farm 24,000 acres.
August 1	Corvallis Lumber Co. Retail Department closes.

August 1	TECO becomes testing agency for Western Veneer & Plywood and Willamette National.
September	Green veneer plant installed at Carlton (closed 1961).
December	Willamette National merges with Willamette Valley. Yew Creek Logging (Benton Co.) merges with Willamette National.
1958 / September	Plywood plant at Willamette National opens.
November	Wenatchee, Wash. sheet plant opens (burned 1967).
1959	Hammond Tract acquired. McLeod Tree Farm (11,148 acres).
February	Compton, Calif. corrugated container plant opens.
May	Sweet Home plywood plant opens (Santiam Lumber).
October	George T. Gerlinger Park given to Polk County.
1960 / July	Construction completed on office building for WVLCo. in Dallas.
September	Leased Kalof properties (subsequently purchased)—2 container plants in Vernon (combined into Cerritos in 1974), Richmond medium mill and container plant (closed 1971), Port Hueneme medium mill (closed, reopened 1965). Cadillac Container in Port Hueneme closed prior to acquisition.
December	Wood Fiberboard (Duraflake) begins production.
1961	Last use of railroad at Black Rock. Lebanon Plywood opens.
May	Sacramento opens as a sheet plant.
June	Gerlinger Park dedicated by Polk County Park & Recreation Commission.

September	Beaverton, Ore. bag plant opens.
1962 / April	Rainbow Lake / Indian Park Ranch deeded to Yamhill County.
July	Dallas small log mill opens.
July	Mill Creek Park given to Polk County.
August	Second growth harvest begins at Black Rock.
1963	Mohawk Veneer (Springfield Plywood) built.
	Second production line added at Duraflake.
January	Sacramento installs a corrugator.
February	Elk Grove, Ill. corrugated container plant opens.
August	#2 paper machine begins operating at Albany.
August	Pak-Rite Division acquired (sheet plant) (sold 1970).
December	Meadow Lake Camp donated to Cascade Area Council of the Boy Scouts.
1964 / January	Western Kraft purchases an interest in Druth Packaging Corp. (sold in 1969).
November 5	Brooks-Willamette incorporated.
November 19	Santiam Southern formed.
1965 / January	Brooks-Willamette buys Tite Knot & Dahl Pine (sawmill and plywood plant kept by Brooks-Scanlon when Brooks-Willamette split in 1977).
Spring	Willamette forms Earn and Learn Scholarship Program.
March	Santiam Lumber Co. Lebanon sawmill closes.
April	Rebuilt Port Hueneme paper mill opens.
June 30	Mohawk Veneer merged into Santiam Lumber Co.
July	Paint line installed at Duraflake.

November	Santiam Southern opens.
November	WesCor formed.
1966	Foster scrag mill opens.
	Wimer Dallas shop opens.
March	Brooks-Willamette particleboard begins production of KorPINE.
March	Haynesville, La. veneer plant opens.
May	McGowan Creek Park donated to Lane County.
June	Springfield Plywood completed.
October	Los Angeles Bag opens.
November	Rockford, Ill. leased plant opens (closed 1969).
1967	Sheathing plant completed for Brooks-Willamette at Redmond (Brooks-Scanlon takes in 1977 split).
March 3	Merger creating Willamette Industries, Inc.
March 31	Willamette acquires 81% of Wimer Logging.
May	WesCor (Corrugating Medium Mill) opens 50% Corco, 50% Western Kraft (wholly owned in 1977).
May	Purchase of Lulay Bros., Scio, Ore. 3,373 acres.
June	Aurora, Ill. corrugated container plant opens.
June	Bellevue, Wash. corrugated container plant opens.
August	Fire burns Wenatchee, Wash. sheet plant replaced by office and warehouse only.
October 19	50% of Dodson, La. plywood purchased.
December	Folding Carton Division of Flintkote acquired.
1968	Duraflake HMC developed.
	First lands purchased in Tennessee.

January 19	Albany Building Materials Group Administrative offices open.
May	Mable Picnic Area donated to Lane Co.
1969	Folding carton plant constructed in Camarillo, Calif. to replace old Flintkote plant.
January	Beaverton business forms plant opens.
June	Bleached hardwood pulp mill (Kentucky) begins productions.
September 10	Woodard-Walker-Willamette incorporated.
1970 / February	Western Kraft East corrugated container plant opens in Bellmawr, N.J.
March	Woodard-Walker-Willamette (Minden, La.) begins making plywood.
April	Second line added at Bend, Ore. particleboard plant.
May	Third production line added at Duraflake.
September 22	Duraflake South incorporated.
December	Willamette acquires outstanding minority (19.8%) interest in Western Kraft.
1971	Third paper machine installed at Albany.
September 8	Wilmar Plywood incorporated.
December	Davis Bros. & Pardee purchase of southern timberlands (70,000).
1972 / February	Duraflake South begins making particleboard.
May	Operations begin at Wilmar (Natchitoches, La.).
June	Buy Rex (Philomath) Veneer and 19,500 acres from Mr. and Mrs. Rex Clemens - start up 1/73.
July	Los Angeles Bag moves to Buena Park facility.
September	Custom Products opens in Albany, Ore.

October 2	Headquarters moves into First National Bank Tower (First Interstate Tower).
November	Red River paper mill groundbreaking at Campti, La.
December 28	Purchase Hunt Lumber Co. [Columbia, (closed in 1975), Dodson, Danville, Zwolle].
1973/September	Beaverton Ink Plant opens.
1974	Bauman purchase: Lebanon Lumber, Lebanon Machine, Bauman Sawmill, WJH Trucking, Indianola Sawmill.
February	Vernon operations phased out, Cerritos, Calif. corrugated container plant opens.
March	Garrigus retail chain leased: McMinnville, Newberg, Lincoln City, Forest Grove, Sherwood (closed 1976).
June	Willamette purchases remaining 50% of Wilmar.
June	Red River begins linerboard production.
October	Willamette purchases Johns-Manville timberland in Jarrett, Va. Willamette exchanges the Virginia timberland for Louisiana timberland (34,000 acres).
1975	Mobol Products purchased by Brooks-Willamette Corp. (merged with Custom Products in 1978).
February	Eastern Forms opens at Langhorne, Pa.
August	Pittsburgh, Pa. (closed 1979) and Riegelsville, N.J. corrugated container plants purchased.
September	Independence retail yard closed.
October	Duraflake FR introduced.
1976	Lumber treating plant constructed at Zwolle, La.
February	Dallas/Ft. Worth corrugated and bag plant opens.

December	Tigard, Ore. yard acquired. Opens May, 1977.
1977	Kortron EB introduced.
April	Brooks-Willamette splits. Willamette keeps the particleboard plant; Brooks Scanlon keeps the Redmond sawmill and plywood plant.
May 27	Corco merger completed: Bowling Green, Delaware, Grand Rapids, Huntington, 50% WesCor, Muncie (closed 1978).
1978	Totem Building Supplies in Vancouver, Washington acquired.
March	Bolinger Lumber Co., Ltd. lands purchased 21,500 acres in northern Louisiana.
May	Emerson, Arkansas sawmill purchased.
June	Ink plant opens at Delaware, Ohio.
July	Zwolle plywood opens.
November	Mauser's retail store at The Dalles, Oregon, acquired.
1979	Willamette Trucking (Sweet Home, Ore) purchased.
March	Moses Lake, Wa. Corrugated opens.
April	Midwest Forms opens, Indianapolis, Ind.
May	Bowling Green corrugated moves to new facility.
June	Plastic bag plant opens in Norwalk, Calif.
August	Dallas/Ft. Worth bag moves to new facility.
December	Emerson, Arkansas plywood opens.
1980	Construction begins on fine paper machine at Hawesville, Ky.
	Ground broken for construction of business forms plant in Dallas/Ft. Worth area.

| February | Buy Woodard-Walker Lumber Co., with plywood plants at Minden and Taylor, Louisiana, 50,000 acres. |
| April | Cerritos, California business forms plant opens. |

Graphic Design: Design Council, Inc.
            Byron Ferris, Charles Politz, Letha Wulf
Set in Sabon, designed by R. Hunter Middleton
Typography: Metro-Portland Typesetting